THE TRUTH ABOUT SPIRITUAL WARFARE

THE TRUTH ABOUT SPIRITUAL WARFARE

YOUR PLACE IN THE BATTLE BETWEEN GOD AND SATAN

C. MARK CORTS

NASHVILLE, TENNESSEE

Printed in the United States of America

Ten-digit ISBN: 0-8054-4389-4
Thirteen-digit ISBN: 978-0-8054-4389-9

Published by B&H Publishing Group
Nashville, Tennessee

Dewey Decimal Classification: 235.4
Subject Heading: SPIRITUAL WARFARE \
CHRISTIAN LIFE \ SPIRITUAL LIFE—GROWTH

1 2 3 4 5 6 7 8 9 10   10 09 08 07 06

This book is dedicated to the many faithful members of Calvary Baptist Church in Winston-Salem, North Carolina.

Through the nearly forty years I shepherded this church, they prayed for me, supported me, and worked side by side with me to build a great congregation for God's glory.

May God bless the future ministry of this church in such a magnificent way that all those who come to be part of it in the ensuing years know that this is where spiritual warfare took place and God's people, through the power of the Holy Spirit, came out on top.

I give praise to the Lord for the victories won and the enemy that was slain during my ministry there.

CONTENTS

ACKNOWLEDGMENTS

THROUGHOUT MY YEARS of ministry as pastor of the Calvary Baptist Church of Winston-Salem, North Carolina, I was blessed to have many kind and encouraging people who urged me to write. As with so many pastors, I found it challenging to find the time for anything more than preparing, writing, and preaching messages amidst a schedule filled with the needs and demands of a growing fellowship.

When I did find time to invest in writing other materials, I gave myself to evangelism and discipleship materials that would specifically develop the dear people whom God gave me to shepherd. Finally, now in my retirement, God has allowed me the time, the help, and the opportunity to turn my attention to the task of writing a book on a subject that has been of vital interest to me as a pastor and of great importance in my own walk with God. I am glad to share with the larger body of Christ the principles on spiritual warfare I have gleaned from the Scripture and practiced in my own life.

This book was originally a series of sermons preached to the congregation at Calvary Baptist Church under the heading of "Spiritual Warfare." These precious people, who were my one and only congregation for forty years, not only heard the reality of spiritual warfare but watched it played out before them in my life time and again. They have stood by their pastor faithfully and prayerfully over the years, and I can say of them, as Paul said of the Thessalonians, "You are [my] glory and joy" (1 Thess. 2:20).

Many thanks are due Mrs. Martha Jones, my writing assistant and coordinator of this book. Martha diligently poured herself into making this book a reality, cleaning up manuscripts and coordinating the efforts of my skillful and kind editor, Reverend William Kruidenier.

To my dear wife, Shirley, more is owed than words can express. I am so grateful to our Lord for giving me such a strong, supportive partner in the joys and sorrows of ministry. Neither of us knew what we would face as we embarked on the work God gave us. Through it all, we learned to trust His heart and take the spiritual conflict that accompanies ministry seriously. And I have learned from her the meaning and full measure of a "steadfast love" that can stand not only the storms of life that can be seen but also the spiritual battles that cannot be seen.

—C. Mark Corts
Winston-Salem, North Carolina

FOREWORD

SPIRITUAL WARFARE IS AS OLD as the garden of Eden. Actually, spiritual warfare predates the creation of man. In Isaiah 14:12–15, we are introduced to a cosmic struggle between Lucifer and Jehovah. In the New Testament, Jesus seems to allude to this event when He says, "I saw Satan fall like lightning from heaven" (Luke 10:18). Throughout the Bible the purposes of God battle the desires of Satan. These are played out on the stage of the human drama. In Revelation 20:10, the outcome of this spiritual battle is revealed when Satan is "cast into the lake of fire . . . and will be tormented day and night forever and ever."

While there is no question about the outcome of the spiritual battle between God and Satan, there are many questions about how man interfaces with this cosmic struggle. Some spiritual warfare books have created more heat than light. *The Truth about Spiritual Warfare* focuses on the light revealed in Scripture. Using historical, biblical illustrations, Dr. Corts allows the reader to see what is going on beyond the physical realm.

One of the central insights of this book is that spiritual warfare does not pit human strength against satanic attacks. It is not a battle between man and Satan but between Satan and God. Though man is often the focus of Satan's attacks, Satan's purposes do not have to do with the defeat of man but the desire to supplant God. This is good news for the Christian who feels overwhelmed with spiritual oppression. The battle is not ours but the Lord's.

I know of no one more qualified to write on the subject of spiritual warfare than Dr. Corts. He writes out of nearly forty years' experience as pastor of the same local church but also the experience of intense physical pain. He is a living example of the apostle Paul's statement, "When I am weak, then am I strong" (2 Cor. 12:10). Facing overwhelming physical problems over the last fifteen years, Dr. Corts has drawn on the power of the all-sufficient Christ.

It was my privilege to serve with Dr. Corts for thirty-two of those thirty-nine years in which he was pastor of Calvary Baptist Church. I have greatly admired his faith, perseverance, and deep confidence in the purposes of God even when those purposes were not revealed. Three times I have seen him come back from the jaws of death and in the power of Christ continue his ministry. The truth about spiritual warfare shared in this book has been part and parcel of his own spiritual journey.

I take great delight in commending to the reader *The Truth about Spiritual Warfare*. It is my prayer that this volume will be used by God to encourage the pilgrims of the next generation to look "unto Jesus, the author and finisher of our faith" (Heb. 12:2).

—Gary D. Chapman, Ph.D.
Winston-Salem, North Carolina

WHAT I SAW AS I BEGAN PREACHING my Easter Sunday evening message on March 31, 1991, struck me as odd but not sinister. After all, it was the day before April Fools' Day. Was this an ill-timed joke of some sort?

The woman dancing around and chanting in the back of our church was unusual for our congregation, to say the least. But we are not a legalistic fellowship by any means, and if this sister in the Lord felt led to pray and dance as I preached, who was I to quench the Spirit? I was aware of her dancing but not aware that she was praying to Satan to destroy me. However, she was disturbing the people in the back pew and a private investigator in the service ushered her out.

I discovered later that the woman dancing and praying as I preached was not a sister in the Lord. And the events that unfolded following that night convinced me that this woman's actions set in motion a season of suffering in my life—suffering that I attribute directly to the most intense kind of spiritual warfare wherein Satan attacks the work of God through a servant of God on earth.

Before I tell you who this woman was and the impact she had on my life—and how God intervened to save me in the midst of a fierce battle—let's consider suffering in a way you may not have before.

Why Do We Suffer?

Erich Maria Remarque's *All Quiet on the Western Front* painted a picture of World War I that startled readers with its graphic details of war. The story was told through the eyes of Paul Baumer, an enlistee in the German army. His experiences in the German army boot camp raised the question of the purpose of suffering—until he realized its purpose for himself:

> I have remade [my commander] Himmelstoss' bed fourteen times in one morning. Each time he had some fault to find and pulled it to pieces. I have kneaded a pair of prehistoric boots that were as hard as iron for twenty hours—with intervals of course—until they became as soft as butter and not even Himmelstoss could find anything more to do to them; under his orders I have scrubbed out the Corporals' Mess with a tooth-brush. Kropp and I were given the job of cleaning the barrack-square of snow with a hand-broom and a dust-pan. . . . With full pack and rifle I have had to practice on a wet, soft, newly ploughed field the "Prepare to advance, advance!" and the "Lie down!" until I was one lump of mud and finally collapsed. . . . I have stood at attention in a hard frost without gloves for a quarter of an hour at

> a stretch, while Himmelstoss watched for the slightest movement of our bare fingers on the steel barrel of the rifle.

Paul Baumer could not have been faulted for asking *why* in the face of such (seemingly) mindless exercises. But he soon discovered his own answer: "Had we gone into the trenches without this period of training most of us would certainly have gone mad. Only thus were we prepared for what awaited us. *We did not break down, but adapted ourselves*" (italics mine).

What appeared to be pointless suffering to a recruit paid valuable dividends for a soldier under fire. Besides preparation for future testing, there are other biblical reasons for suffering.

Peter says that when we suffer for the sake of Christ, "the Spirit of glory and of God rests upon [us]" (1 Pet. 4:14). Christ gets glory when human beings are willing to identify with Him in spite of being persecuted for doing so.

Paul reasoned that his personal suffering was to keep him from becoming prideful about his apostolic privileges (2 Cor. 12:1–10). There's nothing like a permanent thorn in one's sole to slow the step of a prominent apostle (or preacher).

Isaiah offered a unique view of suffering when he said that the sinless Servant of the Lord suffered for others: "He was wounded for our transgressions, He was bruised for our iniquities; the chastisement for our peace was upon Him, and by His stripes we are healed" (Isa. 53:5). Parents sometimes suffer when their children sin, for example.

More reasons for our suffering are found in Scripture (see John 9:3—so that the works of God might be revealed). The one I want to focus on seems rarely discussed: sometimes we suffer as a direct result of spiritual warfare.

Behind the Curtain in Job

Natives in Africa say, "When elephants fight, the grass gets trampled." That's what we see happening in the Book of Job—the clearest look behind the curtain in the Bible. Two titans, God and Satan, were engaged in warfare, and Job was the grass that got trampled.

Here's the key point in understanding suffering as spiritual warfare: Satan was not attacking Job—he was attacking God. Satan's goal was to discredit God (de-glorify God) by showing that God's most loyal subject on earth, Job, would curse God and blame Him if things went badly in his life. Satan said, "God, I don't believe your most loyal follower thinks enough of You to stand by You if all his blessings are removed. Give me access to Job and I'll prove it."

Job suffered terribly on earth as a result of something going on in heaven. But he remained faithful without understanding; sometimes we are faithless in spite of our understanding. Like Paul Baumer on the German front, Job did not break down but adapted—in spite of what he didn't understand. He adapted by enduring. How much more faithful should we be since we have the written account of what happened in heaven and on earth. We know why Job was being attacked and therefore why we might be as well.

Again, ultimately Satan is not after me, he is after God. Satan wants God's position: "I will be like the Most High" (Isa. 14:14). If Satan attacks Job or attacks us, it is ultimately to tarnish the image of God among the heavenly hosts. The story of Job is the story of suffering as spiritual warfare.

Job was "the greatest of all the people of the East" (Job 1:3), a wealthy man with seven sons and three daughters.

He was fabulously wealthy but did not allow his wealth to come between himself and God. He was "blameless and upright, and one who feared God and shunned evil" (Job 1:1).

Satan had access to both the courts of God and the courtyards of man. It was from "going to and fro on the earth, and from walking back and forth on it" (Job 1:7) that Satan entered the presence of God and accused Job of being faithful only because he was blessed. "Remove the blessing and the hedge of protection," Satan suggests, "and Job will not be the faithful one You imagine him to be."

When the angels ("sons of God," Job 1:6) present themselves to God, it is in the form of a heavenly council, gathered to do His bidding. I picture them like the prophet Micaiah did in 1 Kings 22:19—"the host of heaven standing by, on His right hand and on His left." Hebrews 1:14 tells us that angels are "sent forth to minister for those who will inherit salvation." It is in the council of the Lord that they receive their assignments from God. "Praise the Lord, you his angels, you mighty ones who do his bidding, who obey his word. Praise the Lord, all his heavenly hosts, you his servants who do his will" (Ps. 103:20–21 NIV). And it is into this heavenly council that Satan most likely strode confidently to accuse Job of duplicity—of being faithful in the good times and faithless in the bad.

Natural vs. Supernatural Suffering

Before looking closely at Job's experience, let's clear up something right away: suffering in this life is not always a case of "the devil made me do it." Consider at least four natural reasons for suffering in this life.

1. The distribution of inherited weaknesses—or "bad genes," for short. Human beings have been living in a sin-wrecked world for thousands of years, passing on the accumulated collections of dysfunctional and damaged genes and cells that are inherited and redistributed with each new generation. I find it amazing that, by the pure grace of God, our bodies work as well as they do, given the collective abuse they have suffered over millennia.

2. The disobedience of spiritual law—or "you reap what you sow." God told the Israelites in the Old Testament (Hosea 8:7), and repeated it for us in the New Testament (Gal. 6:7), that if you sow the wind, you're going to reap the whirlwind. Sometimes we suffer because we try to live in God's world apart from His laws.

3. The disregard of natural law—or "gravity still rules." You can drink yourself to death, eat yourself to death, or bungee-jump yourself to death. You can live like a fool and suffer like a fool and bear full responsibility for it, or get in step with the natural laws that govern God's creation.

4. The disruption of nature for all—or "moan-and-groan syndrome." The apostle Paul says we live in a world that is moaning and groaning under the weight of the curse of sin (Rom. 8:22). The creaking of our bones when we get old is a just a minor echo of the creaking of creation at large. Physicists call this condition *entropy*—the ever-increasing decay and disorder of natural systems. Things naturally break down and fall apart—including us.

Those four reasons for suffering are perfectly valid and I mention them to contrast Job's suffering, and perhaps yours. Supernatural suffering is spiritual-warfare suffering—when Satan launches a direct assault on us for the purpose of discrediting God in the courts of heaven. That's what he did to Job, and it may be what he has done to you.

A Fight in Three Rounds

If it's true that God tests His real friends more severely than the lukewarm ones, then W. E. Sangster, a British minister, was a good friend of God. During the 1950s Sangster began to notice some irritation in his throat and the failing use of one leg. A doctor diagnosed him as having an incurable disease that caused muscular atrophy. Sangster would gradually lose the use of all his muscles, his voice would fail, and he would be unable to swallow.

Accepting the diagnosis, Sangster threw himself into his work supporting British home missions. He planned on a gradual transition to a ministry of writing and prayer, which he did along with organizing prayer cells throughout England. Eventually, his legs became useless and he lost his voice completely. His last tool was his pen, shaky though it was. On Easter morning, just a few weeks before he died, he wrote a letter to his daughter, in which he said, "It is terrible to wake up on Easter morning and have no voice to shout, 'He is risen!'—but it would be still more terrible to have a voice and not want to shout."

Job lost a lot at the hands of Satan, but one thing he didn't lose was his voice. And he used it to defend himself and God against his "friends" who tried to convince him he was being punished by God for some sin.

Here's how the fight unfolded.

Round One: Attack on Job's Family and Property (Job 1:13–22)

Satan got permission from God to take away everything Job had except his wife and his own life. All of Job's ten children and his thousands of livestock were killed by natural calamities or carried off by neighboring raiders.

Remember: there is a method to this seeming madness. Job believed that God was responsible for all his prosperity, so, Satan reasoned, the only way to discover whether Job worshipped God or worshipped what God had given was to take it all away. Yet this was an attack on God, not Job.

Spiritual warfare is always, first and foremost, an attack on the credibility of God. The battleground is the lives of God's followers—that is where the battle is won or lost. So rather than taking something *from* Job, God is handing something *to* Job—an opportunity to confess before heaven and earth that God is greater than the blessings He gives; that God is worthy of praise simply because of who He is.

So what does Job do? He wins round one: "'Naked I came from my mother's womb, and naked shall I return there. The LORD gave, and the LORD has taken away; blessed be the name of the LORD.' In all this Job did not sin nor charge God with wrong" (Job 1:21–22).

Defending the character of God is at the heart of the matter when suffering is a result of spiritual warfare. Satan wants to kick you so hard that you'll blame God. But Job didn't, and I hope you won't either.

Round Two: Attack on Job Himself (Job 2:1–10)

Satan was unimpressed with God and Job's mutual admiration pact (Job 2:3), accusing Job of swapping allegiance to God for the preservation of his flesh and bones: "Stretch out Your hand now, and touch [Job's] bone and his flesh, and he will surely curse You to Your face!" (Job 2:5). So God allowed Satan to afflict Job's body, but Job didn't strike back.

Job was covered with skin diseases from the top of his head to the soles of his feet. His wife assumed they were incurable and advised him to "curse God and die!" (Job 2:9). But Job won round two the same way he won round one: "'Shall we indeed accept good from God, and shall we not accept adversity?' In all this Job did not sin with his lips" (Job 2:10).

Think about losing your health in a day when there was no such thing as health care. The best Job could do was take a piece of pottery and scrape the boils that covered his body. But in spite of the physical pain and agony Job was going through, he would not blame God for his trouble. Job could not believe that the God who had showered blessings upon him was somehow no longer good simply because the blessings had disappeared.

Are you seeing the nature of suffering when it flows out of spiritual warfare? The goal of Satan is for the saint of God to discredit the person of God. You will be attacked, but it is God who stands to lose as the heavenly hosts wait to hear the confession that comes from your mouth in times of trouble.

Round Three: Attack by Job's "Friends" (Job 2:11–37:24)

The one thing Job didn't lose was his voice. He put it to good use for the next thirty-six chapters, defending himself against four so-called friends—Eliphaz, Bildad, Zophar, and Elihu—who tried to convince him that his condition was due to his sin. They weren't out of bounds suggesting that idea (though they had no proof). The general rule in the Old Testament was that "a curse without cause shall not alight" (Prov. 26:2). But we know from Scripture that this was an exception to the rule—Job was, in fact, blameless.

Well, almost blameless. It was true that Job hadn't sinned against God. But it was also true that he had put God in a box. His theology didn't allow for what was actually taking place—that he could be under attack from the devil. It never crossed Job's mind that there could be a "gray" area in which God did things Job couldn't understand. So beginning in chapter 38, Job goes to school with God as the teacher. God never condemned Job's character anywhere in chapters 38 through 42, but He did give Job lessons in the theology of "I'm God and you're not." He didn't condemn Job's impatient demands for answers, nor did He give Job answers. He just focused on reminding Job of who God is—*the very issue that is at the heart of all spiritual warfare.*

God reminded Job that He is worthy to be worshipped even if He never dispenses a single blessing to any of His children. The creation itself declares the glory and greatness of God, a lesson Job was taught in detail. He finally lost his speech—he didn't utter a word for four chapters, until he confessed, "I have heard of You by the hearing of the ear, but now my eye sees You. Therefore I abhor myself, and repent in dust and ashes" (Job 42:5–6).

Job repented not of sin but of having too small a view of God. And in doing so, he won round three of the fight. Satan destroyed Job's family, property, and health and tried to destroy his confidence in God through the accusations of his friends. But Job held on to the end. He never asked God for healing or cursed God for his situation. All he ever wanted was justice, but once he saw God clearly, he stopped asking even for that.

A proper view of God is more important than any possession or any level of self-confidence. And because Job came to that conclusion, he was victorious in the spiritual warfare that came against him. God did restore Job's fortunes, but only after

Job made his confession of repentance, which is all God wanted: to be properly valued before the heavenly court that had listened to the accusations of Satan, the accuser.

When You Suffer

Take these eight insights away from Job's experience in spiritual warfare:

1. Your suffering is not punishment for sin. Jesus Christ suffered once and for all for sin, so that you and I don't have to. You may be undergoing spiritual warfare, but you are not being punished for your sin.

2. God wants to use you to bring glory to Himself in spiritual warfare. Your confession of allegiance to God is as important as anyone else's.

3. You are in good company. If Satan attacks you, you stand in the company of Job and many others who have been similarly targeted. Your job is to stay in their company by remaining faithful to God regardless of what comes (Heb. 11).

4. It takes endurance to win in spiritual warfare. James refers to Job's endurance when he exhorts the church to endure in suffering (James 5:11).

5. The key to victory is cooperating with God. When you recognize that your suffering is a matter of spiritual warfare, relax. Don't fight it or run from it. You know something is happening that involves you bringing glory to God, so stay in the flow and be faithful while the battle is worked out in heavenly places (Dan. 10).

6. In spite of our weakness, we can be victorious. Job demonstrated, without knowing what we know about spiritual warfare, that it is possible not to curse God when you suffer. Given what we know, we should do even more, allowing God to be our strength when we are weak (2 Cor. 12:7–10).

7. God does not forsake those who are fighting for Him. Throughout Job's questioning and impatience, God never left him. He came to Job in the end and showed him what he needed to know. And He will never leave or forsake you (Heb. 13:5).

8. There are no easy answers in spiritual warfare, only insights. If we call out to God when we are suffering, He will answer us. He may not tell us everything, but He will give us insight into the battle raging around us (Jer. 33:3).

The Rest of the Story

Remember the woman who was dancing around and (I thought) praying as I preached that Sunday evening message in March 1991? It would be months later that I discovered she was a disciple of Satan, praying that I and my ministry would be destroyed. Several days after that Sunday while preaching in St. Louis, Missouri, I suffered a massive heart attack.

I was taken to a small hospital in St. Louis where the doctors clinically "lost" me. Reviving me, they decided around 11:00 p.m. to transfer me to a larger hospital with better facilities. By about 5:00 a.m. the next morning, I was stabilized. But it wasn't until November 1991 that I received compelling evidence of the spiritual warfare I was involved in.

After telling a brief version of the March 1991 events on television in November 1991, I received a letter from a pastor in another city in my state. In this letter, he revealed how he had heard about the television broadcast in which I told the story of the woman praying down curses upon me, my heart attack, and the touch-and-go situation that ensued for several days thereafter. The heart attack occurred on a Friday night, and this pastor's church had been praying for me all during that weekend.

On Monday night, three days after the heart attack, this pastor was awakened in the middle of the night in the grip of an evil presence. He immediately got out of bed and began to intercede for his family when my name came to his mind. He knew he was to pray specifically for me, and his wife awoke and joined him. He continued to pray on through the early morning hours until he sensed a measure of peace about my condition, at which time he returned to bed.

The next day, however, he heard that I had taken a serious turn for the worse, and his church continued to pray. His letter was to tell me that he did not believe my heart attack was purely a medical problem but a manifestation of a spiritual conflict. At the time he was called from his bed to pray for me, neither he nor his church knew anything of the woman who had been praying curses against me in our church. That part of the story was only made public in the November broadcast. But when he heard about the story I had shared on television, it all made sense to him. He knew the Lord had used him to enter into a spiritual conflict on my behalf. He knew my physical suffering was not just a medical event but a spiritual event manifested physically.

He closed his letter with these words: "That night was a very strange time to me. With what I now know, things do not seem quite so strange anymore. I praise our Lord for the weapon of prayer. May God's hand continue to abide [with] you and your family as you boldly proclaim Jesus Christ in the days ahead."

How thankful I was, months after my heart attack, to learn that God had been marshalling spiritual forces to deliver me from the clutches of death and the curses of the enemy through the power of prayer. God received the glory as we stood fast and waited and watched for God to give Himself the victory over the attacks of the evil one.

Not all suffering is due to spiritual warfare. But when you discern that it is, you must defend the honor and name of God with all your heart, soul, mind, and strength. All of heaven is watching to see whether you will be faithful to continue to praise God in spite of what you can't see or understand.

Discussion Questions

1. Several reasons for suffering were mentioned in this chapter: to prepare for further testing, to bring glory to Christ, to produce humility, to undergo the effects due to the acts of others. What other biblical reasons or causes for suffering can you identify?

2. In what realms have you seen the proverb "When elephants fight, the grass gets trampled" realized? In church? Family? Business? What caution should this bring to those in authority?

3. What correlation might there be between the faithfulness of Christians and their attractiveness to Satan as a battlefield for spiritual warfare (for example, Job)? Explain.

4. How much natural suffering in this life could be avoided by the application of wisdom (for example, the impact of lifestyle issues—diet and exercise—on sickness)? How do you think God responds to prayers for relief from suffering when the suffering is self-inflicted?

5. Do you believe that true spiritual warfare is an attack by Satan upon God, played out on the battlefield of human lives? What are the implications of that truth for being victorious in spiritual warfare?

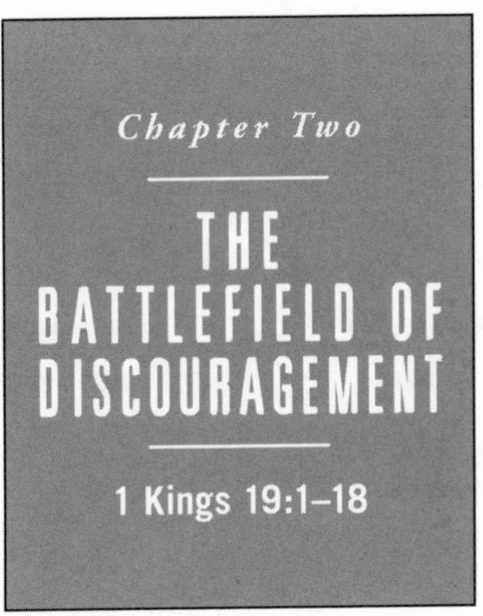

Chapter Two

THE BATTLEFIELD OF DISCOURAGEMENT

1 Kings 19:1–18

IN HIS BOOK *DOWN TO EARTH,* John Lawrence tells about the day the devil advertised all his best tools for sale. There was great excitement over the items that appeared: Hatred, Envy, Jealousy, Doubt, Lying, Pride—they were all there. One tool, however, lay apart from the rest. It seemed harmless enough, though it was well-worn and had a price that greatly exceeded the rest.

> "The name of that tool?" asked a shopper.
>
> "That is Discouragement," replied the Adversary.
>
> "And why is it priced so high?"
>
> "Because it is more useful to me than the others. I can pry open and get inside a person's heart with that one when I cannot get near him with other tools. Once I get inside with Discouragement, I can make him do whatever I choose. See how worn it is? That's because I use it more than any other tool. I use it on almost everyone because *very few people know it belongs to me.*" (italics mine)

Are you one of the vast majority of Christians who never thinks of discouragement as a tool of Satan? If you are, then you run a great risk of harming the name of God both in heaven and on earth. You are learning in this book that spiritual warfare is primarily between Satan and God, not Satan and man. When Satan seeks to bring shame and reproach to the name of God, he attacks those who will speak against God when they lose confidence in Him. And discouragement can bring you so low that you become vulnerable to even further attacks from the devil.

Dissect the word *discouragement* and you have *dis*—a prefix that means "the absence of" or "the opposite of"—and *courage*—that state of mind that allows you to face life's negative circumstances with confidence. So discouragement is the absence or opposite of a confident state of mind. Once your confidence in God goes, you open the door to a host of other attacks from the enemy of your soul.

If you are a Christian, Satan's war against God is won when you conclude that God has deserted you, no longer cares about your circumstances, or has turned a deaf ear to you. At that moment, you do the opposite of worship. Worship is ascribing worth to God, which we too often do on the basis of what He has done for us. If you conclude that God has stopped doing for you what you think you need (or want), you conclude that He is not worthy of your faith, confidence, or loyalty.

That represents a victory for Satan—having one more person, in full view of heaven and earth, who has stopped believing in God.

Whether discouragement is Satan's chief tool or not, I cannot prove. But I do know, from experiences in my own life and decades of shepherding God's flock, that discouragement is a wolf in sheep's clothing. It appears harmless and benign but can ravage the human heart. Who doesn't feel a little blue almost daily? Who doesn't feel let down when expectations go unmet? Who doesn't lose their edge when trying to slice through the thicket of challenges life offers on a daily basis?

No one. Everyone is tempted by discouragement. And because we yield to it so easily—not recognizing it for the destroyer it is—we think it's a normal part of life. But it shouldn't be if we understand it for what it is.

Disappointment vs. Discouragement

Kevin Costner's film career was launched with a movie called *Silverado* in 1985. But that opportunity came only as a result of Costner's response to a major disappointment. He had been given a key part in *The Big Chill* (1983), turning down the lead role in another movie. But in the editing process for *The Big Chill,* all his scenes were cut except for a few moments when he appeared as a corpse in a casket during the opening credits. Not exactly the big break he was hoping for.

Lawrence Kasdan, the director of *The Big Chill,* met with Costner to apologize for having to cut Costner's scenes due to the movie being too long. He was shocked at Costner's attitude: "Larry, this has been the experience of my life. It has shown me what kind of actor I want to be, and I wouldn't trade it for anything. You have nothing to apologize for—you have given me a great gift."

Kasdan was so impressed that he knew immediately Costner was an actor he wanted to work with again. Two years later he cast Costner in a lead role in the western *Silverado*—and the rest is movie history.

Don't be confused: disappointment is not discouragement. In Costner's case, *dis-appointment* meant the absence of an appointment. He didn't get to appear in the movie. But it did not lead to *dis-couragement*—the absence of courage. Disappointment is an event; discouragement is an extended attitude. Every time you experience a momentary disappointment, Satan is there, ready to attack God if you fall into discouragement and lose faith in Him.

What does it take to view an event as a gift instead of as a reason for discouragement? I don't know anything about Mr. Costner's internal motivations, but for the Christian I do know what it takes: confidence that every event in life is filtered through the gentle hands of a loving God who gives nothing but good gifts to His children (Rom. 8:32; James 1:17). In Costner's case, it appears his attitude was at least partly responsible for getting another opportunity with the same director—an opportunity that launched his career.

The Character of Discouragement

First Kings 19 records a classic case of spiritual warfare that reveals the character of Satan and how he attacks. It's the aftermath of the contest between Elijah and the prophets of Baal on top of Mount Carmel: the battle of gods—the God of Abraham, Isaac, and Jacob versus Baal, the false god of the apostate northern kingdom of Israel. Baal worship had been entrenched in Israel by the influence of Jezebel, a pagan woman who was the wife of Ahab, the king of Israel. To please Jezebel, Ahab built a temple to Baal in Samaria (1 Kings 16:32) and allowed nearly 850 false prophets of Baal and Asherah to eat at Jezebel's table (1 Kings 18:19). She killed as many of the true prophets of God as she could and had tried to kill Elijah, searching high and low for him (1 Kings 18:4, 10).

Elijah forced a confrontation between God and Baal on Mount Carmel where God won a stunning victory (1 Kings 18:16–46). As a result of this victory, Jezebel pledged to destroy Elijah within twenty-four hours—and Elijah fled for his life.

Disappointing? Of course—no one enjoys being threatened with death. But discouraging? Elijah shouldn't have been, given what he had just seen God do at Mount Carmel. But instead of maintaining his courage, he fled the scene and fell into a serious state of discouragement—even depression.

How did that happen? The same way it can happen to you and me: Elijah failed to separate truth from error and found himself totally discouraged. A sure sign of spiritual battle is when you start believing lies instead of the truth and begin doubting reality and God.

Get familiar with the following four manifestations of Satan's character of discouragement.

1. The distortion of truth. When King Ahab reported to Jezebel about what had happened on Mount Carmel, he got it all wrong: "And Ahab told Jezebel all that *Elijah* had done" (1 Kings 19:1, italics mine). All that *who* had done? It was God who proved Himself the only powerful God by raining down fire from heaven, not Elijah. Satan's first objective is always to leave God completely out of the picture or to credit the work of God to man.

When something bad happens to you and your first thought is to blame another person, you have bought into the deception of Satan. Jesus Himself called Satan "a liar and the father of lies" (John 8:44 NIV). Satan never wants you to see him behind the evil in this world. He wants you to blame another person, or more especially, God Himself.

2. The dissemination of fear. Jezebel put out an all-points bulletin for the murder of Elijah and the prophet was consumed with fear: "And when [Elijah] saw that, he arose and ran for his life, and went to Beersheba" (1 Kings 19:3).

Jezebel was a powerful woman who was toying with Elijah. He was right there at Carmel—she could have had him killed easily. But her goal, in addition to killing Elijah, was to discredit Elijah's God. Remember: God had just won a victory on the mountain. Jezebel, by announcing her intent to kill Elijah, was giving him time to decide whether his God could come through a second time. If the people of Israel got word that the man of God was running from a worshipper of Baal, what would they think of God? Spiritual warfare is always about discrediting God, which is what Jezebel wanted to do through Elijah. She succeeded with her threat, for Elijah turned tail and ran for his life.

There are only two possible ways to respond to the future: in faith or in fear. The future, by definition, deals with what is not known. We don't know what the next twenty-four seconds will bring, much less the next twenty-four hours. The question is, how will we approach the future, the unknown? With faith or with fear?

The opposite of faith is not unbelief; it is fear (Matt. 8:26). So the quickest way for Satan to discredit God is to neutralize faith, and the quickest way to neutralize faith is to inject a lethal dose of fear into the patient. That's what Satan did to Elijah and that is what he will do to you and me. There is no faith in the presence of fear, nor fear in the presence of faith. We will reveal one or the other when confronted with the unknown in life. And since God has not given us a spirit of fear (2 Tim. 1:7), where do you think it comes from?

3. The distraction of issues. The third manifestation of Satan's character comes when he confuses the issue—when he gets Elijah's attention off the real issue and onto Elijah. And see how quickly it can happen: Elijah has just been through a dramatic event in which God was the issue. Elijah had been faced with an unknown on Mount Carmel: would God manifest Himself and burn up the sacrifice and demonstrate His power? Elijah exercised faith, soaking the wood with water and taunting Baal, believing God would show up in fire and fury—which He did. It was all about God on Mount Carmel—but now Elijah had made it all about himself.

I have driven the 115 miles from Mount Carmel in the north to Beersheba in the south, and it is not an easy trip even in a car. But Elijah *ran* the entire way—and then went another day's journey into the wilderness—so energized was he by fear. This was a case of fear-induced adrenalin; there was nothing spiritual about it. Elijah forgot about God, made his own safety the issue, and ran for his life.

The safest thing we can ever do is to "abide under the shadow of the Almighty," making Him our refuge and fortress (Ps. 91:1–2). When we fail to do that—when we make life all about us instead of all about God—that's a sure sign of spiritual warfare.

Satan is still using distraction today. The alcoholic thinks his wife is the problem. The teenager thinks his parents are the problem. The church thinks the pastor is the problem, and the pastor thinks the board is the problem. When someone else is the problem, it's easy to justify our discouragement. We can't change others, so we're justified in remaining discouraged.

When you find yourself losing sight of God in some circumstance—you're protecting yourself by blaming others and running away in fear—you're in the middle of a spiritual battle. God's honor and reputation are always the only issue. Satan wins when we allow him to distract us with side issues.

4. The destruction of confidence. In the wilderness, Elijah was ready to turn in his prophet's mantle and call it a career: "It is enough! Now, LORD, take my life, for I am no better than my fathers" (1 Kings 19:4). He had just seen God empower the destruction of 450 of Jezebel's prophets but now was convinced that Jezebel was about to kill him. If this is not a true case of *dis-couragement*—the absence of courage and confidence—I don't know what is.

If you've lost sight of truth, are scared to death, and have stopped focusing on God, what are you left with in life? Elijah had come to the logical conclusion of his own thought processes. The ultimate victory for Satan—remember, his goal in spiritual warfare is to discredit God—is for God to kill his primary prophet. So that's the thought Satan puts in Elijah's mind: "Now, Lord, take my life."

Whenever someone's confidence is so totally destroyed that they see no conclusion but to die, you know you're dealing with spiritual warfare. God always edifies and builds up; Satan always discourages and tears down.

God wants you to be confident about many areas of your life—marriage, parenting, career, faith—including your estimate of your own value and worth in God's eyes. If your confidence is found in God, you will not become discouraged. That doesn't mean you won't fail or sin. It means that because you are making God the issue instead of yourself, you will remain confident. He never fails—so why would you lose confidence in Him?

In 1893 Rowland Bingham arrived in Lagos with Walter Gowans and Thomas Kent to evangelize sub-Saharan Africa. They were told, "Young men, you will never see the Sudan; your children will never see the Sudan; your grandchildren might see the Sudan." Undeterred, they set out on an eight-hundred-mile journey into the interior of the continent, but in less than a year, both Gowans and Kent were dead. From England Bingham returned to Africa where he later wrote, "My faith was being shaken to the very foundation."

Seven years later Bingham had established the Sudan Interior Mission and set out from England for Africa again. This time he almost died from a case of malaria. Discouraged, his companions returned to England, and Bingham, in his weakened state, had no alternative but to follow them. Following this effort he wrote, "It would have been easier for me, perhaps, had I died in Africa, for on the homeward journey I died another death. Everything seemed to have failed. . . . I went through the darkest period of my whole life."

In 1902 Bingham made his third attempt and this time succeeded, establishing the first Sudan Interior Mission station in Africa. Today SIM (Serving in Mission) serves in more than forty countries from nine worldwide bases of operation.

Was Rowland Bingham disappointed at times? Without a doubt. Did he battle discouragement? Absolutely. But in the end he did not lose sight of truth, give in to fear, or focus on the wrong issues. Millions of people populate heaven today from all over the world because he remained confident in God.

The Character of Encouragement

Just as Satan's character is revealed in the ways he attempts to discourage us, so God's character is revealed in the ways He encourages us. We saw that the prefix *dis* means "the absence of or opposite of." What about *en*? It means "to put into or onto, to cover or provide with, to cause to be." It's easy, then, to see what *en-courage* means. When God encourages, He puts courage in us, provides us with courage, causes us to be courageous. God does for us what the great Dallas Cowboys running back Emmett Smith did for one of his friends in the NFL.

In 1994 the Buffalo Bills lost the Super Bowl for the fourth year in a row. Their star running back, Thurman Thomas, had fumbled the ball three times. After the game, Thomas sat alone on the bench, head down, devastated and discouraged. Staring down at the ground with his face in his hands, he saw a pair of football shoes stop in front of him. He looked up and saw that the shoes belonged to the Cowboys' Emmett Smith, who was holding a little girl.

"Thurman," Smith said, "I want you to meet my goddaughter." Then, turning to the little girl, Smith said, "Honey, this man right here is the greatest running back in the NFL."

Like a laser beam cutting through the mist, Emmett Smith's words cut through the fog of his friend's discouragement. The idea that a peer whom he respected would take a minute to give him an encouraging word meant the world.

It's one thing for a peer to encourage you, but another thing for the God of the universe to *en-courage* you. But encouragement is God's role in your life. Discouragement is the manifestation of the character of Satan; encouragement is the manifestation of the character of God.

Mark well these four ways God will work through you to defeat the attacks of Satan.

1. The accommodation of strength. Elijah was in the desert, desiring to die. But God came to him to take away his discouragement. The manifestation of God's character will be the same in your wilderness as it was in Elijah's.

Elijah fell asleep and an angel appeared with food for him to eat. He ate and fell asleep again. He then ate a second time. With strength from that food he walked forty days and nights to Mount Horeb, the mountain where God first appeared to Moses in the Sinai desert. In Elijah's case, strength from encouragement came from food from God. Physical health and strength are critical factors in maintaining spiritual and emotional health.

Whatever we need—physical strength, a friend, finances, an opportunity, counsel—God will use it to encourage us in the midst of spiritual warfare. Jesus didn't need food for His forty days in the wilderness (Matt. 4:1–11), but Elijah did. Whatever "desert" we are in, God will bring the encouragement we need.

2. The appearance of God's presence. Note that there is no record of God telling Elijah to journey to Mount Horeb. Elijah was still trying to get even further away from Jezebel, the cause of his fear. God's question to Elijah, when He found His prophet hiding in a cave, points out that He didn't direct His prophet to the cave: "What are you doing here, Elijah?" (1 Kings 19:9). The man who had called down fire from heaven and killed four hundred fifty prophets of Baal was hiding in a cave.

When Elijah offered a self-centered, fearful explanation, God arranged to reveal Himself to His prophet to encourage Him. First the mountain was rocked by a great wind, then an earthquake, then fire—but in none of those Carmel-quality manifestations was the Lord to be found. It was in "a still, small voice" that followed the wind, earthquake, and fire that Elijah heard God again ask, "What are you doing here, Elijah?" (1 Kings 19:13)

Elijah was so discouraged that he failed to see the opportunity God was giving him to repent of being confused by the issues. The prophet again lamented that he was the only prophet left in Israel who had not bowed the knee to Baal, and that he was about to be killed. Elijah didn't have eyes of faith to see what was going on. He couldn't see that God, not Elijah, was the issue.

If you are a child of God, be prepared for God to come to you if you are yielding to discouragement. He may come through a friend, through the pages of Scripture, through a song, through a Bible teacher on television, or through a book. And He will more than likely come in a still, small voice—so you must have ears to hear and eyes to see if you are to be encouraged by His presence.

3. God's appointment to action. To get Elijah out of the cave and out of his doldrums of discouragement, He gave him a plan. He was to appoint new kings over Syria and Israel and a new prophet to take over Elijah's role. Sometimes taking action is what we need to get our minds off our circumstances. Even vigorous exercise—which causes endorphins, the body's own natural mood enhancers, to be released in the brain—can change our whole outlook.

When Cain was downcast and discouraged, having brought an offering to God that was displeasing, what did God tell him? "Why has your countenance fallen? If you do well, will you not be accepted?" (Gen. 4:6–7). If you do wrong, get up and do right. It might be work, reconciliation with another, an act of repentance, ministry, exercise—you decide. But sitting and sulking is not likely to be effective in defeating discouragement.

4. Association with the godly. The last way God encouraged Elijah might have been the most important of all. He revealed there were seven thousand more prophets in Israel just like Elijah who had not bowed the knee to Baal (1 Kings 19:18). Whether seven thousand is a literal number or a symbolic round number, the point was this: Elijah was not alone.

When God told Adam in the beginning, "It is not good that man should be alone" (Gen. 2:18), He spoke something fundamental about the nature of humanity: we are social beings as well as individuals. Our fallen, introspective tendency is to isolate ourselves when discouragement is a temptation—exactly the opposite of what we should do. We need to find a prayer partner, a network, a friend, a spouse, or a small group. God uses others to encourage and build up the body of Christ.

If you are looking for God to deliver you from discouragement with something as dramatic as a hurricane, an earthquake, or a wildfire, I have news for you. It rarely happens that way. Yes, it happened that way in the pages of the Gospels and Acts, and there were good reasons for God's using dramatic encounters in those days. But we are talking about spiritual warfare here, not point-in-time conversions of lost souls.

Wars start slowly and they end slowly. World War II was essentially over with the invasion of Normandy by the Allied forces on June 6, 1944. But the surrender of the Japanese did not occur until August 15, 1945—more than a year later. Spiritual warfare is not unlike physical warfare. Hold your ground and defend the name of your God against the attacks of the enemy, listening for the still, small voice of God as time passes.

The weapons of your spiritual warfare are not those of this world, but they are mighty nonetheless, adequate for "pulling down strongholds, casting down arguments and every high thing that exalts itself against the knowledge of God, bringing every thought into captivity to the obedience of Christ" (2 Cor. 10:4–5). With God's encouragement you will win the battle by believing the truth instead of lies, looking to the future with faith instead of fear, staying focused on God instead of self and others, and keeping your confidence in God.

May these words of the great Reformation theologian, John Calvin, serve you well in your battle against discouragement:

> The wisest servants of God sometimes weaken in the middle of the course, especially when the road is rough and obstructed and the way more painful than expected. How much more, then, should we ask God that He never withdraw the aid of His power among the various conflicts that harass us, but rather that He instill us continually with new strength in proportion to the violence of our conflicts.

Discussion Questions

1. What are the chief sources of discouragement in your life—things that cause you to lose courage or confidence in God? What strategic advantage do you have in knowing what your sources of discouragement are?

2. How consistently are you able to keep disappointment (the absence of an expected result) from becoming discouragement (the absence of courage)? What is the best way to keep the former from becoming the latter?

3. Fear, not unbelief, is the opposite of faith. How have you seen this to be true in your life?

4. What correlation do you find in your own life between discouragement and lack of attention to physical and spiritual health? In times of stress, what should you be alert for?

5. Who serves as a resource for you when you are discouraged? Why is a spiritual partner a strong defense against attacks on your courage?

Chapter Three

FEAR AS SPIRITUAL WARFARE

2 Timothy 1:7

ONE OF THE MOST ACKNOWLEDGED fears that we have learned from experience is the great number of people who fear public speaking. Jerry Seinfield once observed that, if indeed it is a major fear among people, when a man dies he would actually prefer to be in a coffin than at the pulpit delivering the eulogy.

What surprised me very much was that in many lists of phobias I could not find a particular phobia that the Bible mentions prominently: the fear of man. However, I did find listed the "fear of people or society" (anthropophobia) and the "fear of men" (androphobia, arrhenphobia, or hominophobia—usually referring to males as opposed to females, though sometimes used generally). But the term found in Proverbs 29:25—the "fear of man"—is missing on lists of phobias. That verse says, "The fear of man brings a snare, but whoever trusts in the LORD shall be safe."

We can think of the *fear* of man just like we think of the *fear* of the Lord, referring to honor, reverence, and respect. The question is, do we honor man more than we honor God?

Once when the apostle Paul was exhorting the church in Galatia, he established the tension between fearing man and fearing God this way: "For do I now persuade men, or God? Or do I seek to please men? For if I still pleased men, I would not be a bondservant of Christ" (Gal. 1:10). Paul obviously did not fear man more than he feared God.

The fear of man causes human beings to do desperate things. A male biology professor at a Florida university admitted to having inappropriate sexual contact with three female students. When the affairs came to light, school officials asked the young women why they had not reported the encounters. They replied that they were afraid the professor would punish them with poor grades.

Those girls were caught in a snare: "Do I run the risk of getting a bad grade, even failing the course, or do I report the professor?" They obviously were more fearful of what the professor might do to them than they were of the shame of inappropriate sexual contact. "The fear of man brings a snare."

The reason we know that fear of any kind—but especially the fear of man—is a weapon of our enemy is because of Paul's words to his young protégé, Timothy: "Therefore I remind you to stir up the gift of God which is in you through the laying on of my hands. *For God has not given us a spirit of fear*, but of power and of love and of a sound mind" (2 Tim. 1:6–7, italics mine). As a young pastor in his first full-time assignment in Ephesus, Timothy was stepping onto a battlefield and Paul knew it. (Yes, the church can be a place of spiritual warfare.) Paul knew that whatever fear and apprehension Timothy felt were not from God. And if God is not the source of our fears, guess who is. Because the fear of man is the opposite of the fear of God, there is nothing Satan would like better than to convince us to live in fear of man—or any of the other five-hundred-plus fears, for that matter.

The second part of Proverbs 29:25 says, "But whoever trusts in the LORD shall be safe." Can you imagine Satan strutting around before the throne of God in heaven pointing out this and that Christian on earth, who really fear a multitude of things more than they fear God? Remember—in spiritual warfare, attacks on us are really attacks on God. It is God whom Satan seeks to dethrone, and he uses attacks on us to make God look bad in heaven and on earth. If you have ever heard a voice in your head say, "I thought God promised to keep you safe and meet your needs. You don't look too safe to me. In fact, you look pretty scared. Where is God when you need Him?" you know you're involved in spiritual warfare.

Seven Deadly Fears

There are seven deadly fears that can snare us if we walk into them, and all of them have their roots in the fear of man. To be victorious in the battle against fear, you must know how to identify these snares when you encounter them.

Fear of Loss

The more valuable something is, the greater the temptation to succumb to fear of its loss. In Genesis 26 we read about Isaac succumbing to the fear of losing his most valuable possession, his wife, Rebekah. When Isaac and Rebekah went into Philistine territory because of a famine in Canaan, Isaac was afraid that the Philistines would kill him and take his beautiful wife. He didn't trust in the Lord; he lied about who Rebekah was—"She is my sister." But when the Philistine king, Abimelech, looked out the window one day and saw Isaac caressing Rebekah, he confronted Isaac. Isaac had to confess his fear of death and his lie, and Abimelech, far from killing Isaac, told the Philistines not to touch Isaac or Rebekah. "Anyone who molests this man or his wife shall surely be put to death," Abimelech ordered in Genesis 26:11 (NIV). Now Isaac's days under Abimelech were nearly completed. Isaac planted crops and reaped a hundredfold because the Lord blessed him. He became rich and his wealth continued to grow until he became very wealthy. The Philistines, then envious of his many flocks, herds, and servants, filled all of his father Abraham's wells with earth. "Then Abimelech said to Issac, 'Move away from us; you have become too powerful for us'" (Gen. 26:16 NIV). Isaac moved away and encamped in the Valley of Gerar. He reopened the wells his father Abraham had opened there. Then Isaac and his men opened new wells. As he trusted and obeyed God, his fear of loss was overcome by God's provision of new wells. As in the case of Rebekah and then the wells, if we trust in the security of those things, we may lose them. However, our own trust in the living God overcomes our fear of loss and gives God an opportunity to prove Himself and His provision.

If there is something we love so much that we are not willing to trust God with it, then our love for that object has become greater than our love for God. The theological term for what we must do is *renunciation.* We are not renouncing our love, desire for, or affection for the object or person. We are renouncing our attempt to control what happens. We decide to do right and trust God for the results.

Fear of the Wicked

The psalmist David experienced the fear of the wicked in a way that is easy to identify with in our day:

> Deliver me, O LORD, from evil men;
> Preserve me from violent men,
> Who plan evil things in their hearts;
> They continually gather together for war.
> They sharpen their tongues like a serpent;
> The poison of asps is under their lips.
> Keep me, O LORD, from the hands of the wicked;
> Preserve me from violent men,
> Who have purposed to make my steps stumble.
> The proud have hidden a snare for me, and cords;
> They have spread a net by the wayside;
> They have set traps for me. (Ps. 140:1–5)

We don't know specifically what David feared, but the crusade of King Saul against him comes to mind. Paranoid and psychotic, King Saul tried to kill David. When he failed, Saul tried to assassinate David's character among his countrymen. David had good reason to fear the wicked. But look at how he responded:

> I said to the LORD: "You are my God;
> Hear the voice of my supplications, O LORD.
> O GOD the Lord, the strength of my salvation,
> You have covered my head in the day of battle.
> Do not grant, O LORD, the desires of the wicked;
> Do not further his wicked scheme,
> Lest they be exalted." (Ps. 140:6–8)

Every fear is a test of faith in which you ask yourself, *Will I do the wrong thing or will I put my trust in God?*

Norma McCorvey, the Jane Roe of *Roe v. Wade* (the Supreme Court decision that made abortions legal in America), decided she had feared those in the pro-abortion movement long enough. She decided to put her trust in God, saying that "the people in the pro-life movement have loved me in a way that those in the pro-choice movement have never loved me, but have only taken advantage of me." She finally decided that her fear of what others would do to her if she followed her conscience was something she could entrust to God.

Fear of the Crowd

In Isaiah 8, the prophet is given a message for the apostate northern kingdom of Israel: "The riches of Damascus and the spoil of Samaria will be taken away before the king of Assyria" (verse 4). Because that was clearly an unpopular message for a prophet to deliver, God gave Isaiah a warning about succumbing to the pressure of the crowd:

> "Do not say, 'A conspiracy,'
> Concerning all that this people call a conspiracy,
> Nor be afraid of their threats, nor be troubled.
> The LORD of hosts, Him you shall hallow;
> Let Him be your fear,
> And let Him be your dread." (Isa. 8:12–13)

If prophets are not immune to the temptation to fear the majority opinion, what does that say about the rest of us?

Instead of fearing the crowd, we'd best fear the Lord and let Him be our "dread." Crowds act like a wheat field, the tall stalks of grain swaying in unison with every change of the wind. Those who join crowds are the same way. They fear the judgment of the crowd, should they decide to "sway" a different way. We can't fear God and the crowd at the same time (Matt. 6:24).

I spoke out publicly on an issue with moral implications coming up for a vote in our community. A man in my church told me that his coworkers had noted my public involvement and criticized it, saying a preacher should confine his voice to the pulpit. Where would this world be if men and women of God, especially those in pastoral leadership, had not taken a moral stand on the public issues of their day?

Fear of the crowd will silence the voice that does not fear God.

Fear of Pain

If you watch much television these days, you may be convinced that it is now possible to live a pain-free life—at least to a degree. Supposedly no longer do we have to suffer with the pain of headaches, backaches, sore muscles, acid reflux, heartburn, allergies, or arthritis. Men have even been freed from the emotional pain of not being able to enjoy intimacy with their wives. We live in a culture that will do just about anything to avoid pain.

Jesus Christ had some telling words for His followers about the fear of pain: "Do not fear those who kill the body but cannot kill the soul. But rather fear Him who is able to destroy both soul and body in hell" (Matt. 10:28). He sets up the juxtaposition we've seen in every case: the choice is whether to fear man or to fear God.

If someone is bringing pain into your life, how you respond will be a function of whom you fear most: God or the person inflicting the pain. If you fear the latter, you will kowtow to him or her in hopes that the red-hot poker in your eye will be withdrawn. But if you fear God, you will find yourself numbered among those who were "stoned . . . sawn in two . . . tempted . . . slain with the sword . . . [who were] destitute, afflicted, tormented—of whom the world was not worthy" (Heb. 11:37–38).

Fear of Failure

In the well-known parable of the talents in Matthew 25:14–30, the master severely upbraids a servant in whose possession he had left a single talent to be invested. That servant was afraid to invest his talent in some enterprise that would benefit the master for fear he might fail and be punished. So he dug a hole and hid his talent in the ground—and got rebuked for his decision when the master returned.

How many ministry positions in your church—Sunday school teacher, nursery worker, sports coach, choir member—are going unfulfilled because people are afraid of failure? People don't want to step forward and volunteer to serve because they are afraid of failing and the embarrassment that follows.

The quickest way to defeat the fear of failure is to confess the sin of pride. It is our inherited propensity to self-protect that keeps us on the sidelines of life. And that is a victory for the enemy when it comes to spiritual warfare. Both victory and defeat regarding fear are seen in the encounter of the disciples with Jesus when He approached them walking on the water (Matt. 14:22–33). Peter conquered his fear, if not permanently, while the rest of the disciples cowered in the boat.

When a reporter asked Jonas Salk how he handled the two hundred failed attempts to create a polio vaccine before succeeding, he said, "I never had a failure in my life. I learned two hundred ways not to make a polio vaccine, but I never had a failure." And when someone asked Winston Churchill about flunking the second grade, he replied, "I didn't fail. I was given a second chance at the same grade."

A lot of success stems from perspective. Everyone who succeeds fails at some point, but they don't consider themselves failures. They view the occasional failure as a lesson in how not to achieve their goal. Victory in spiritual warfare occurs when we believe that God rewards faithfulness, not success versus failure. Knowing we will be rewarded for faithfulness (for trying) frees us up to leave the results to God.

Fear of Losing Face

What happens when we lose face? It means we lose power, influence, position, or popularity. Call it what you will—we all fear it. Nobody wants to be thought of as a "loser."

The Pharisees in Jesus' day certainly didn't. They were being shown up consistently by the peripatetic carpenter from Nazareth who was followed and adored by crowds wherever He went. In Mark 12 we have Jesus' parable about a vineyard owner (God) who left his vineyard (kingdom) in the hands of tenant farmers (the Pharisees). The farmers killed the owner's messengers (prophets) and ultimately his son (Jesus) when they came to get an accounting of the vineyard. In the end, Jesus said, the owner will punish the tenant farmers and give the vineyard (kingdom) to others who can manage it effectively (Gentiles and other non-Pharisee Jews).

How would you have felt if you had been a Pharisee listening to this indirect condemnation? Mark 12:12 tells us exactly how they felt: "And they sought to lay hold of Him"—and not with the hands of blessing. So why didn't they? Because they "feared the multitude, for they knew He had spoken the parable against them. So they left Him and went away." The Pharisees were losing face with the people and they knew it.

On a trip to Israel I saw a beautiful ring I wanted to buy for my wife. The vendor wanted $30 for it but we bargained the price down to $24, and I bought it. I was proud of my negotiating skills and showed the ring to several people in our group. But when we got back on our tour bus I discovered another man had bought the same ring for only $18! I immediately lost face with those to whom I had boasted about my "great price." At the next bus stop, I stood back and watched my better-bargainer friend do his thing with a vendor. Then I moved in, intent on out-bargaining this man and restoring my position as the sharpest shopper on the tour.

Just as I started negotiating with the vendor, the Holy Spirit spoke to my heart: "Corts, you're a fool! Why do you let what one man did control your life? If the $24 you paid for the ring was a good price, take it, praise God for it, and don't ever look back. Your standing with Me is not determined by how good a bargainer you are. It's okay to be bested by another."

Fortunately I listened and walked away and never again worried about not being the best shopper on the trip. Unfortunately, the Pharisees didn't walk away and allow Jesus to be who He was—the Son of God. They tried to kill Him because He was making them look bad in front of their constituents. When you find yourself fearful of losing face, go ahead and lose it. Far better to do that than to be snared in issues of pride, envy, and jealousy.

Fear of Rejection

Most everyone is familiar with the famous hierarchy of needs established by Abraham Maslow, the twentieth-century psychologist. He theorized that human beings strive to meet five levels of needs in their lives: first, physiological needs, then safety needs, then love needs, then esteem needs, and finally self-actualization needs. In other words, man's highest fulfillment comes not from meeting material needs but from finding and fulfilling a sense of purpose and achievement. And nothing negates that highest sense of fulfillment like rejection.

Think about the times you have felt most rejected in your life. You were doing something important to you when someone pulled the rug out from under you and caused your self-esteem and self-actualization to crumble. Many people live with the scars of rejection all their lives. And all of us live with the fear of rejection.

But the fear of rejection brings about our old familiar juxtaposition: do we trust God or do we fear man? If we allow man to define us, we will conform to whatever standard will insulate us against further rejection. But if we allow God to conform us into the image of Christ, we can know we are on His timetable and there is no rejection in this world that can derail that process (Rom. 8:29).

When Paul wrote to the church in Philippi from a jail cell, he identified a silver lining in his cloud of imprisonment: "Most of the brethren in the Lord, having become confident by my chains, are much more bold to speak the word without fear" (Phil. 1:14). *If Paul could find joy in a jail cell,* the brethren reasoned, *what rejection do we have to fear?*

Today the church doesn't witness like it should primarily because of a fear of rejection. But if we would compare the laugh, the snide remark, or the indifference we get when we witness with the torture, death, and imprisonment some of our brethren receive in parts of the world when they witness, we would fear rejection a lot less.

If you and I are "accepted in the Beloved" (Eph. 1:6), why do we fear the rejection of man?

Overcoming Fear in Spiritual Warfare

Remember—God has not given us a spirit of fear. To walk in fear is to walk hand in hand with the enemy, not with God. Three commitments on your part will keep you free from fear.

1. Learn to identify ungodly fear. Fear acts like a warning alarm going off within us. When we feel the alarm, our immediate task is to identify the cause. There are all kinds of moral and physical dangers that we should be deathly afraid of, saving us from danger.

But healthy fear is not the fear we're talking about in this chapter. We're talking about the fear of man instead of the fear of God; compromising your beliefs and your spiritual integrity because you fear what man might do to you. That is unhealthy, ungodly fear, and it is not from God. The fear of ruining your marriage by participation in an office dalliance—that fear is from God (2 Tim. 2:22). But the fear of man is not.

Situations that require God's management are usually based in an ungodly fear of man: wheeling, dealing, manipulating, scheming. When I turn things over to God's management, I know I have identified and defeated that carnal fear of man. I trust Him to work it out. I can be passed over, defeated in an election, cut from an athletic team, refused a promotion—it doesn't matter. If I find myself trying to manage those situations (reverse them to my benefit), I am living in fear. If I trust God with those events, I live in peace.

2. Focus on the truth of Scripture. We have already noted the most important truth concerning fear in spiritual warfare: fear of man does not come from God but from Satan. When you hesitate to bow your head and pray before a meal in a restaurant because you fear what people will think, where does that fear come from?

Paul says in Romans 8:15 that we "did not receive the spirit of bondage again to fear, but you received the Spirit of adoption by whom we cry out, 'Abba, Father.'" Keeping your Abba God central in your life will allow you to live in His protection. Keep these Scriptures in mind for fearful situations:

- "Do not be afraid . . . for the LORD will be your confidence" (Prov. 3:25–26).
- "Do not be afraid . . . I am your shield, your exceedingly great reward" (Gen. 15:1).
- "I will fear no evil; for You are with me" (Ps. 23:4).
- "I sought the LORD, and He heard me, and delivered me from all my fears" (Ps. 34:4).
- "Whenever I am afraid, I will trust in You" (Ps. 56:3).

3. Remember that perfect love casts out fear. The apostle John tells us a day is coming when all the evil and wickedness of men will be judged. Christians will stand boldly in that day without any fear of judgment because of the love of God: "Perfect love casts out fear. . . . But he who fears has not been made perfect in love" (1 John 4:18).

When we understand God's perfect, unconditional, loyal love for us, we do not need to fear anybody or anything. We can take to heart the words of Jesus when He walked on water to the disciples: "Be of good cheer! It is I; do not be afraid" (Mark 6:50). Stop and think for a moment: can you imagine any situation in which you would be fearful if Jesus Christ was standing right next to you? I can't—not a single one. And the reality is that He is with us moment by moment, having promised never to leave us or forsake us (Heb. 13:5). The simple presence of Jesus overcomes fear.

Recently one of my adult daughters confessed one of the great sins of her childhood. She said, "Daddy, when we used to take long trips and we would come home, I would lay in the back seat and play like I was asleep, just so you would have to put your arms underneath me and pick me up. I loved to have my daddy carry me up to bed and put me to sleep."

If my arms provided security and peace to my daughter, think how the perfect, loving arms of our Father God can cast out fear from our lives.

Fear in spiritual warfare brings us to the brink of a decision: will we fear man or trust God? How we answer that question determines the outcome of the battle.

Discussion Questions

1. In the human realm, whom do you fear in an inappropriate way? (Family members? Professional peers?) What impact does this fear have on your life?

2. What things in life do you fear losing the most? Have you been successful in entrusting those things to God? What factors—objective or subjective—stand in the way of your faith?

3. Do you think the pulpit is an appropriate place for speaking out on the moral issues of our day? Why or why not?

4. Consider the times and places you have failed in your life. Have those failures made you fear failure, or are you OK with it, should it come again? Explain.

5. How much do you fear losing face with your peers—being bested by them in some arena? What should you do to conquer this fear?

Chapter Four

AT THE END OF THE ROPE

1 Samuel 24:8–17

ON AN EASTER SUNDAY MORNING several decades ago, everything was going perfectly. All four of our little children had on their Easter finery and were ready to go to church. Shirley and I were coiffed and dressed to the nines, very much the proud Easter parents. The morning weather was warm but glorious—a perfect beginning to a great day of worship and celebration.

As I prepared to pull the car away from the house, I heard the voice of eight-year-old Amy: "Daddy, what are we going to do about the little chickens?"

Someone had given Amy three little Easter chicks that she was keeping in a pen in the backyard. Somewhere in the far distant regions of my mind, I began to feel uneasy about what might be coming next.

"I knew we were going to be at church a long time today, so I let them out of their pen to get some exercise," Amy explained innocently.

Maintaining my Dad-of-the-year demeanor, I said, "No problem, honey. You all sit here in the car and stay cool, and I'll get the chicks and put them back in their pen."

Famous last words. I found the chicks scratching around in the woods behind our house, and every time I bent over to grab one, it would "cheep cheep" and scurry out of my grasp. I was losing the battle, not only with the chicks but with myself. I was panting and sweating and getting more frustrated by the minute. The cologne, deodorant, hair spray, and starch were all melting in a rain of perspiration. Within minutes I was soaking wet, looking like Moses coming down from the mountain with a mop on his head.

Time was running out—Shirley and the children were going to be late for Sunday school. So I went back to the car and told her to go on to church while I tried again to round up the chicks. And to add insult to my injured pride, they drove off snickering over my bedraggled appearance and frustrated tone of voice. I was sweating like a linebacker while those I was serving were sitting in air-conditioned comfort, laughing at me. It might have been funny, but I was in no mood to be laughed at.

I eventually returned the chicks to their pen but had to get myself showered and groomed again. I arrived at church just in time to preach with a whole new appreciation for the need of resurrection power on that Easter Sunday.

Only one word could describe how I felt that morning: frustrated—and that's putting it mildly.

Between a Rock and a Hard Place

In no way did my situation that Easter morning compare with Aron Ralston's in May 2003. Aron had gone hiking alone in a Utah canyon without telling anyone his plans. While he was climbing, an eight-hundred-pound boulder shifted and pinned his right arm against the rock wall. He was entirely immobile. And no one knew where he was, and he was low on water and food and was in such a narrow canyon that even a search plane flying overhead would probably never see him. He was frustrated, scared, and desperate.

After five days he knew he had to do something or he would eventually become a skeleton hanging by his forearm on the side of a canyon wall. Taking out a utility tool and tying a tourniquet around his pinned forearm, he broke two bones in his wrist and then proceeded to cut his hand off just above the wrist. Though his forearm had grown numb from the pressure of the boulder, he later admitted that the pain was a hundred times worse than anything he had ever felt before. Walking out of the canyon and back onto well-traveled trails, he encountered a couple who assisted him with food, water, and support. A search helicopter that had been looking for him appeared and ferried him to a hospital where he began the process of recovery.

Later, when Aron was asked how he survived the ordeal and maintained the kind of composure needed to do such a difficult thing, he said, "I was [at first] throwing my body against the boulder trying to see if it would budge at all, but it didn't move. It took some big calm thinking to get myself to calm down and to stop throwing myself against the boulder so that I didn't hurt myself anymore than I needed to."

Frustration as Spiritual Warfare

Admittedly, chasing little chickens around cannot be compared to what Aron Ralston experienced—except in one way:

I had the same potential for injuring myself spiritually as he did physically. He saw that if he didn't stop throwing himself against an immovable boulder, he would hurt himself further. And I saw that if I didn't stop what I was doing and send my family on to church, I might explode in anger. I needed time to calm down and reflect, just as Aron did.

Frustration has the potential for launching a major spiritual battle. Satan would like nothing better than to see us throw ourselves against an immovable situation and hurt others or ourselves in the process—and bring shame upon the God who has promised us the ability to live in resurrection power. Satan loves to see us get to our wits' end:

> They mount up to the heavens,
> They go down again to the depths;
> Their soul melts because of trouble.
> They reel to and fro, and stagger like a drunken man,
> And are at their wits' end. (Ps. 107:26–27)

What he doesn't want us to do is what the psalmist did:

> Then they cry out to the LORD in their trouble,
> And He brings them out of their distresses.
> He calms the storm,
> So that its waves are still.
> Then they are glad because they are quiet;
> So He guides them to their desired haven.
> (Ps. 107:28–30)

Frustration happens to everyone in this life, and we will never be free from it. The question is what we will do when we face it. We can either be defeated by it or be victorious over it. If we hurl ourselves against the cause of our frustration, we lose and

Satan wins. But if we "cry out to the Lord in [our] trouble," God wins and the devil loses.

I have found six responses to frustration in Scripture: three are negative and three are positive. Which category of response we choose will determine the outcome of the spiritual battle we're in.

Giving In to Anger

The months and months of harassment David went through after being anointed the new king of Israel provide an example of how not to get angry. In 1 Samuel 24, David refuses to stretch out his hand against Saul, the Lord's anointed king—an amazing example of self-control in the face of unbelievable frustration. Regardless of what David did right, Saul hounded him from one end of Israel to the other. A lesser man would have speared the bull when caught on the horns of such a dilemma.

In the next chapter, however, David didn't fare as well—anger and revenge in the face of frustration almost consumed him. After making a measure of peace with Saul (1 Sam. 24:21–22), David moved with his followers to the wilderness of Maon. There, a surly Calebite named Nabal lived with his beautiful and intelligent wife, Abigail. He was extremely wealthy, with huge herds of livestock and many shepherds. David had once looked out for Nabal's shepherds and treated them fairly. On that basis, David sent a party of his men to Nabal to ask for whatever provisions he might provide for them. Nabal, however, was less than appreciative of David's actions and sent David's men packing—empty-handed.

David's immediate response was to prepare for battle. If Nabal was going to be true to his name (which means "fool"), then David would treat him accordingly and teach him a lesson

—and get the food he needed for his men. In the meantime, Abigail learned of her husband's ungrateful response to David and intervened. She loaded donkeys with provisions and went to meet David on his way to kill Nabal. She begged him not to sully his own name and the name of God by taking vengeance on a fool, deserving as Nabal might be.

Abigail's intervention defused a classic case of spiritual warfare spilling over into the affairs of men. How would it have looked for God's newly appointed king, the young David, to fly off the handle and murder a fool who insulted him? That's where David was headed before Abigail stepped between him and Nabal.

David's anger was the "short-fuse" type: an explosion that happens so fast it's almost impossible to stop. You come around a corner in life and slam into a frustrating person or situation and—BAM!—you've said or done something you live to regret. That's what David would have done if Abigail hadn't stopped him.

The other kind of anger is the "long-fuse" kind. This happens when you brood over something for hours or days. You haven't lashed out so you think you've got your feelings under control. And then months later, the same person who frustrated you originally does something simple that offends you and you blow up all over them. All that stored-up anger finally comes roaring out.

Think of the spiritual and physical warfare Abigail prevented by her calming words to David. And think of the disappointment Satan must have felt when she intervened. Though he would fail later in his reign as king, for the moment David would remain the anointed king and not be branded a murderer. And

God's promises to David would be kept. But frustration leading to impulsive anger was almost the undoing of David.

Frustration is a stronghold of Satan in the mind of man and we feel imprisoned in it. But God promises that there is always a way out—and anger is not it (1 Cor. 10:13; Eph. 4:26–27).

Surrendering to Frustration

Another strategy of Satan is to bring you face to face with the worst of yourself, convincing you there's no way out, so your only option is to throw in the towel—to give up on yourself and God. When that happens, one more soldier is removed from the active army of the Lord, and God is made to look unworthy as Commander-in-Chief.

This is what happened to Judas, the traitor among the original twelve disciples. If you recall the familiar story, after Judas betrayed Jesus in the garden of Gethsemane and delivered Him to the Jewish and Roman authorities, he grew remorseful: "I have sinned by betraying innocent blood," he said to the chief priests and elders (Matt. 27:4). He tried to give back the thirty pieces of silver he had earned for his infamous deed, but the authorities wouldn't take it. It was blood money, and nobody wanted it. They told Judas, "Your sin and your blood money are your problem—deal with it!" And deal with it he did—by hanging himself.

Suppose Judas had confessed what he had done to Christ instead of to the Jewish elders? He did the right thing by confessing, but he confessed to the wrong people. That was a sign that Judas was remorseful but not repentant. When we're remorseful, we want someone to tell us it's OK that we got caught doing wrong. When we're repentant, we want someone to forgive us for doing wrong. Should Judas had gone to Jesus and said, "Master, I took money to betray You. I'm truly sorry and I repent of what I've done." We'll never know.

You know when you're in the midst of spiritual warfare by whether you are being destroyed or built up. Satan always wants to bring out the most destructive part of our lives, while God wants to bring out our most constructive parts. Satan tears down; God builds up. Satan wants to box you in and convince you that feeling remorseful ("I'm sorry I got caught") is better than being repentant ("I'm sorry I sinned"). When you've sinned and you know it and you're not willing to admit it, giving up is really your only option since you can't live a duplicitous life as a disciple.

But God doesn't want you to give up when you've been caught between a rock and a hard place. Sure it's frustrating—it's supposed to be. He wants you to agree with Him that you've sinned and accept His restorative grace and continue on. He gets far more glory by forgiving you and restoring you than He ever gets when you walk away.

Embracing Denial

Author and radio humorist Garrison Keillor has said, "Sometimes you have to look reality square in the face and deny it!" That's good humor, of course, but bad theology—and bad practice as well. Truth and reality don't change just because we deny them.

Denial is one of the easiest strategies to identify as a precursor to spiritual warfare. Why? Because of something Jesus said to Peter in Luke 22:31: "Simon, Simon! Indeed, Satan has asked for you, that he may sift you as wheat." Jesus knew that Peter was about to deny Him as a result of an attack from the enemy.

Jesus prayed for Peter that he would be restored after his failure (v. 32), but it was obvious that Peter was about to enter a serious round of spiritual warfare. As with Job, Satan tempts us to bring out the bad in us, while God tests us to bring out the good.

Denial takes two forms. The first is silent: we deny reality with our actions. This is the kind of denial demonstrated by a desert nomad who awakened hungry in the middle of the night. He lit a candle and began eating dates from a bowl beside his bed. The first one he bit into had a worm in it so he threw it away. He bit into a second date and discovered a worm in it as well and quickly threw it away. Reasoning that he would never satisfy his hunger at this rate, he blew out the candle and quickly ate his fill.

This happens to us as well. We deny our mounting debt and continue to spend. We deny our teenager's problems and turn away. We deny our bulging waistline and continue to eat.

The second form denial takes is verbal: faced with the truth, we lie. This is what Peter did three times: "Woman, I do not know Him" (Luke 22:57). Peter had done this earlier when Jesus said it was necessary that He must die and Peter contradicted Him: "Far be it from You, Lord; this shall not happen to You" (Matt. 16:22). This was another instance of intense spiritual warfare, based on Jesus' words: "Get behind Me, Satan! You are an offense to Me, for you are not mindful of the things of God, but the things of men" (Matt. 16:23).

When we are frustrated—boxed in between a rock and a hard place—we either live like it isn't true or say it isn't true. We simply refuse to admit there is a problem. And when we do, Satan gets the glory and we get the grind until we look reality in the face and accept it.

We don't have to give in to frustration. It is possible to respond in a positive way—a way that brings glory to God and victory in spiritual warfare to us.

Waiting on the Lord

Think back to the setting I mentioned earlier—David in the cave where he refused to embarrass or harm Saul, the Lord's anointed king (1 Sam. 24). David respectfully confronted Saul about their situation and then placed the matter in God's hands: "After whom has the king of Israel come out? Whom do you pursue? A dead dog? A flea? Therefore let the LORD be judge, and judge between you and me, and see and plead my case, and deliver me out of your hand" (1 Sam. 24:14–15). David raised the issue—"Why are you pursuing me?"—but concluded by saying he would let the Lord be the judge. David was not about to take matters into his own hands and take vengeance upon Saul.

This was a consistent pattern for David in his prayers in the psalms. He would call upon the Lord to deliver him from the hands of his enemies, but then conclude by saying, "Wait on the LORD; be of good courage, and He shall strengthen your heart; wait, I say, on the LORD!" (Ps. 27:14). Many times, frustration leads to waiting on the Lord. You have respectfully and lovingly confronted another party, and you have taken your case to God—and you are still boxed in. At that point, you have two choices: take matters into your own hands and do something dishonoring to God or wait upon God. Which do you think will result in the preferred outcome in terms of spiritual warfare?

Waiting upon God is an act of faith; it is an act of trust that He sees your situation and is at work to bring about His resolution of it. It may not be peaceful or painless, but it will be perfect if it is His.

Taking Action

Is taking action always wrong? Of course not. An example of taking godly action—affecting a creative solution to a desperate situation—is found in Mark 2.

Jesus was teaching in a house in Capernaum with standing room only. The crowd was spilling out of the house into the street. Sick people, the curious, the committed—the place was packed. When four men approached carrying their paralyzed friend on a pallet, they no doubt grew frustrated at their inability to get him in the presence of the Healer. They could have gotten angry, given up, or become abusive and demanded an audience. But they didn't—they let their need inform their creativity.

You know the story. They carried their friend up the stairs on the outside wall of the house that led to the roof. They began tearing up the dirt and tile roof until they created a hole big enough to lower their friend, on his pallet, into the house. Can you imagine the commotion this must have caused? Dirt and debris falling down onto Jesus and those in the room. People having to move out of the way to allow the pallet a place to land. An upset homeowner (was this Peter's house?)—"Hey, what are you doing to my roof?"

But Jesus was impressed by the faith revealed in their actions. They believed that if their friend was within arm's reach of Jesus of Nazareth, he would be healed. And he was.

Creativity is an untapped element of faith in the Christian church; it's like a surprise attack in spiritual warfare—something Satan never sees coming. Next time you're between a rock and a hard place and getting more frustrated by the minute, pray for creativity. See if you can find a creative solution to the creative situation God has put you in. Where there's God's will, there's a way.

Obeying Faithfully

When a lowly supply clerk in the elite Eighty-second Airborne Division at Fort Bragg, North Carolina, received instructions to participate in a parachute jump, he complied immediately. There was only one problem: he had not yet been trained to jump out of planes. The clerical error notwithstanding, Specialist Jeff Lewis fell into ranks, got his equipment, boarded the plane, jumped out of the plane, and landed on the ground, shaken but unhurt.

When the error was discovered later, his only explanation was that he was doing what a soldier is supposed to do: obey orders. "The Army said I was airborne-qualified," Lewis said. "I wasn't going to question it." May his tribe increase in the body of Christ!

Sometimes God asks us to do something "unreasonable" to free us from our frustrating circumstances: *Lord, I'm not qualified. . . . I don't know how. . . . I'll embarrass myself.* Those thoughts occurred to Moses when God first commissioned him to go to Egypt and lead the Hebrew slaves to freedom (Exod. 3–4). But God's provision for Moses and Aaron seems to have taught him a lesson in obedient faith.

When Moses, following God's direction, ended up between an approaching Egyptian army and the waters of the Red Sea, he decided faithful obedience was the best option. (The fact that it was his only option probably influenced his decisions.) The hundreds of thousands of Hebrews, with their children, their animals, their elderly and infirm, looked back and saw the Egyptian army approaching. They looked ahead and saw the tempest of the Red Sea. And they screamed at Moses, "It would have been better for us to serve the Egyptians than that we should die in the wilderness" (Exod. 14:12). But Moses rose to the occasion, "Do not be afraid. Stand still, and see the salvation of the LORD" (v. 13).

The amazing thing about this situation is that, so far as we know, Moses had no idea what God was about to do. It reminds me of the climactic scene in the zany comedy movie, *The In-Laws*, when Peter Falk, a CIA agent, and Alan Arkin, a dentist, are standing before a firing squad in Mexico. The guns are cocked and the dictator is about to give the order to fire. "You don't have a plan?" Arkin yells at Falk. "I'm open." Falk replies, "What have you got?"

That's faith at work! The bullets are about to start flying, and Peter Falk is expecting a solution to appear at any moment—and it did. And it did for Moses as well, as we know. Moses stretched out his rod over the sea and the waters parted. I'm sure Moses felt just like Specialist Lewis did as he was free-falling out of that plane—eyes wide open, not believing what he was seeing and doing. If Moses were to paraphrase the young trooper, he would have said, "The Lord said I was parting-the-sea qualified. I wasn't going to question it."

Frustration is a huge potential stumbling block in the life of every human being and a battleground in which Satan can attack God through your circumstances. The answer to frustration is not living a problem-free life. That's not going to happen. The answer is to separate the wrong responses—giving in to anger, surrendering to frustration, and embracing denial—from the right responses—waiting on the Lord, taking action, obeying faithfully—and choose accordingly.

When you take the way of escape out of frustration that God provides, you'll get the victory and God will get the glory.

Discussion Questions

1. How would you describe your propensity for anger? What experience have you had with hurting yourself (or others) by your anger?

2. How readily can you find the line that separates legitimate anger from sinful anger? How often does your definition of legitimate anger differ from that of those around you? What is your responsibility in such cases?

3. How would you respond to a person who felt like giving up—quitting the task he or she is involved in (be it marriage, ministry, or another responsibility)? When is quitting the better part of wisdom, and when is it not? What are the criteria?

4. How do you know when you have waited on God "long enough" before taking personal action? Explain the difference between passive waiting and active waiting.

5. Describe the tension between the modern desire to be in control and the life of faith. How do you manage this tension in your own life?

Chapter Five

DECEPTION: SATAN'S FAVORITE TOOL

Jeremiah 17:9

YOU COULD LOOK RIGHT AT a *Portia fimbriata* without seeing it. In fact, you could sit down next to one and brush it away, thinking it was a piece of dried leaf. But *Portia fimbriata* is not a leaf; it is a member of one of the strangest, and most deceptive, species in the animal kingdom. All the *Portia* species are spiders native to the Far East and Australia. Unlike most spiders, the *Portia* spiders are araneophagic—they eat other spiders. And they are chillingly fascinating in hunting their prey.

The *Portia* spiders have conspicuous fans of hairs on their legs and ornate tufts of hair on their body. These clumps of hair give the spider's body an irregular shape, making it resemble a piece of debris instead of a spider—especially when it folds its first three pairs of legs under its body in its normal resting position. This ability to camouflage itself is the *Portia* spider's first level of deception.

It also has three distinct strategies of deception for capturing and devouring other spiders. The first strategy is called "aggressive vibratory mimicry." The *Portia* will climb onto the web of its intended victim spider and begin plucking the strands of the web with its legs. These vibrations tell the host spider that something is trapped in its web. When the host spider approaches to investigate, it finds just a "piece of leaf" blown by the wind. At that moment, the "leaf" (the *Portia*) attacks and kills the host spider.

The *Portia*'s second deceptive strategy is called "nest probing." Certain spiders spin orb-shaped nests. The *Portia* will climb atop the nest of those host spiders and tap with its legs. When the host pokes its head outside the nest to investigate, the *Portia* strikes.

Finally, the *Portia* uses what's called "cryptic stalking." In this strategy the *Portia* follows its intended victim spider very slowly. If the prey turns around to investigate the sound behind it, the *Portia* freezes in place and assumes its debris-like appearance. Getting closer each time, the *Portia* finally is within striking distance and captures its prey from behind.

Think about it—a spider that exists on the basis of deception. I don't pretend to know how to sort that out at the level of the animal kingdom, but I do know this: the enemy of God operates in this world on the basis of deception. As we will see in this chapter, Satan can make himself and his ministers appear as the very light of God.

Deception is a powerful tool in the hand of Satan and a deadly one when overlooked by the Christian. Deception is dangerous for one simple reason: *a deceived person doesn't know he's deceived!* That's the whole point of deception, isn't it? Isn't that why so many innocent spiders get eaten by the *Portia* spider—because they think everything is normal? They see nothing out of the ordinary until they are in the jaws of their attacker. And far too many Christians think everything is normal until they find themselves in the jaws of the one who goes about as a lion seeking whom he might devour (1 Pet. 5:8). Because deceived people don't know when they're deceived, we have to live a lifestyle of sobriety and vigilance.

Satan attempts to deceive Christians into doing things that bring reproach upon the name of God. Remember: spiritual warfare is Satan against God, not Satan against us. And there are four principle areas of our lives wherein Satan longs to dishonor God.

The Heart's Domain

The great Reformed theologian John Calvin said, "Nearly all the wisdom we possess, that is to say, true and sound wisdom, consists of two parts. The first is the knowledge of God, and the second is the knowledge of ourselves." We know far less about ourselves than we think. Jeremiah wrote, "The heart is deceitful above all things, and desperately wicked; who can know it?" (Jer. 17:9).

When a practicing Christian lives an upright life for decades, then suddenly falls into immorality or some other sin, he can spend the rest of his life trying to figure out where that sinful act came from. But that's Jeremiah's point: we don't know our own hearts, the depth of our depravity, of what we are truly capable. The heart is like a *Portia fimbriata*: deceitful—looking one way but acting another. We think our hearts are full of the Spirit and incapable of "desperately wicked" things. When we think that way, it is evidence of the deception in which we live.

What did Jesus say about the heart? "What comes out of a man, that defiles a man. For from within, out of the heart of men, proceed evil thoughts, adulteries, fornications, murders, thefts, covetousness, wickedness, deceit, lewdness, an evil eye, blasphemy, pride, foolishness. All these evil things come from within and defile a man" (Mark 7:20–23). Jesus and Jeremiah were thinking along the same lines.

To follow Calvin's advice, we first pursue knowledge of God. We do that through the study of His Word, through prayer, through the study of His creation where He is revealed, and His acts in the affairs of men. But how do we gain a knowledge of self? There is only one way, and that is through a lifelong process of self-examination. "Know thyself" is good advice, although, with our finite abilities and limited lifespan, we can learn only so much about ourselves. For that reason, I like David's approach in Psalm 139. After describing all the ways God knew him, he then prayed: "Search me, O God, and know my heart; try me, and know my anxieties; and see if there is any wicked way in me, and lead me in the way everlasting" (vv. 23–24). It is far better to ask God, who knows us perfectly and infinitely, to show us our hearts.

To tune your ears to God's examination of your heart, try the following four methods.

1. Know the Scriptures. The apostle James explained why we need to know the Scriptures: because they are like a mirror, revealing the nature and content of our soul (James 1:21–25).

Reading the Bible is not like reading any other book—even a book of purported wisdom and truth. We may gain an insight from other books, but no other book except the Bible is alive: "For the word of God is living and powerful, and sharper than any two-edged sword, piercing even to the division of soul and spirit, and of joints and marrow, and is a discerner of the thoughts and intents of the heart" (Heb. 4:12). The Bible is a living document in the hands of the Holy Spirit. It can pierce into the heart a different way every time we read it. The more we read it, the more we discern "the thoughts and intents of the heart."

Now, apply Hebrews 4:12 to what James says: we are to "receive with meekness" the Word of God. That means we are to sit before the Word with humility and look into it so it may reflect who we really are. If we don't study the Word that way, James says, we are like someone who looks in a mirror but forgets what he looks like as soon as he puts the mirror down. But if we look into the Word with meekness, we will be changed by it. We will become a person whose heart is conformed to Scripture—doers, not just readers (hearers), of the Word.

This part of self-examination doesn't happen in sound bites. It happens in extended times of prayerful, meditative examination of the Word. Only then does the Holy Spirit have opportunity to reflect the nature of our heart back to us as we read God's truth.

2. Know the Holy Spirit. A child learns who he or she is, in part, by interacting with a parent. A child compares what he believes, thinks, and understands with what a parent believes, thinks, and understands. The spirit of the parent is critical in developing the spirit of the child.

In that same way, Paul says, we compare things in our spirit with what the Holy Spirit reveals about God (1 Cor. 2:10–13). The Holy Spirit "knows the things of God," and the spirit of man "knows the things of a man." When we become a Christian, we receive "the Spirit who is from God." In a profoundly mysterious way, the Spirit of God begins revealing to the spirit of man who God is. When we compare who we are to who God is—in terms of holiness, righteousness, expression, and behavior—we come to know ourselves pretty well. And we don't always like what we see.

But it is from that interaction with the Holy Spirit that "he who is spiritual judges all things" (verse 15). And "all things" certainly includes ourselves.

3. Know other Christians. We have become so paranoid in our culture about the matter of tolerance that it has completely negated the positive dimension of a biblical imperative: judging one another and oneself. Granted, we are to "judge not, that you be not judged" (Matt. 7:1). But that has to do with judging unrighteously—judging the speck in a brother's eye when there is a beam in our own or judging someone by our own self-imposed standards. That's the negative, sinful dimension of judging.

The positive dimension of judging ourselves and others is expressed by Paul when he says, "Imitate me, just as I also imitate Christ" (1 Cor. 11:1; also 4:16). Paul considered Christ to be his own model and encouraged others to imitate him, for in doing so they would be imitating Christ. Paul wasn't being egotistical and full of himself. How else are we to know people except by "[considering] one another?" (Heb. 10:24–25). It's absolutely essential to the process of self-examination. All of us are looking for role models and mentors—people whose godly behavior and values we can imitate. When we see such people, we examine ourselves and make necessary changes.

4. Know sin. By knowing God and His Word, we come to know what sin is and what it isn't. Many cultural standards that some Christians have adopted aren't sin (for example, dancing and going to movies) and some practices Christians allow are sin (for example, gluttony and materialism). There is a difference between what is unwise and what is sin, and we need to know that difference. We need to constantly move toward wisdom and away from sin.

When Paul discovered sin in the church at Corinth, he compared it to leaven in bread dough: it will multiply and change the whole "loaf." Therefore, he said to "purge out the old leaven" (1 Cor. 5:7). Christ was sacrificed for the purpose of keeping leaven (sin) out of the church. We are to examine ourselves (1 Cor. 11:28) and excise sin immediately from our lives. The self-examined life must be one of ruthlessness when it comes to sin, whether incidental or indwelling. Proverbs 4:23 tells why: "Keep your heart with all diligence, for out of it spring the issues of life."

To forget that the heart is deceitful is to make ourselves vulnerable to crushing defeat in spiritual warfare. If we ignore God's Word, the Holy Spirit, relationships, and sin, then the self-examined life becomes a self-deceived life. And remember: *the deceived person doesn't know he is deceived.*

The Domain of Wisdom

What trait is shared by a virtuoso violinist, an operatic soprano, and a spellbinding novelist? How about a master plumber, an accident-free trucker, and a high-wire steel rigger? Skill—or in the language of the Old Testament, we would say they shared *hokmah*—the Hebrew word for "skill."

Interestingly, *hokmah* is also translated as "wisdom" in the Old Testament. Therefore, we can easily align "wisdom" with "the skill of living." According to Solomon's proverbs, a wise person is the one who goes through life without running aground on the treacherous shoals of immorality or foolishness; who knows how God would walk through this life and seeks to keep to the same path; who is skilled in understanding, dispensing justice, offering counsel, and solving the riddles of life.

If we are to remain free from the deceptions of Satan, we must not only know our own hearts but also acquire wisdom. In this sense, wisdom is the skill of detecting deception and exposing the trickery and lies of Satan before he is able to enter the sheepfold and kill, steal, and destroy (John 10:10).

There is a famine of wisdom in our land and even in our churches. We have confused intelligence (man's acuity) with wisdom (God's perspective). We emphasize grades and various scores as a measure of intelligence, all the while being deceived by the *-isms* of our day. As a result, we are deceived into thinking that man's ideas can substitute for God's wisdom. As Paul said, "Let no one deceive himself. If anyone among you seems to be wise in this age, let him become a fool that he may become wise. For the wisdom of this world is foolishness with God" (1 Cor. 3:18–19).

The first *-ism* by which many are deceived is *humanism*—the idea that man is the measure of everything in this world, serving as the highest evolutionary order among living beings, and is a moral entity unto himself, unaccountable to any higher authority. It is easy to look around in our culture, and even in some churches, and see the pervasiveness of humanism—that is, the absence of any reference to God.

The Bible, of course, says that God, not man, is the center of everything. Man was created by God and is dependent upon God for his very existence. We were made in His image, which means He is the reference point and standard for our existence as persons in the realm of morals and values. Not to believe this is to be deceived into thinking that life is like a moral and ethical pinball machine—wherever the ball ricochets and lands is the day's definition of wisdom and truth.

The second *-ism* by which many are deceived is *existentialism*, the idea that experience is the measure of truth in life. "If it feels good, do it" is an existential philosophy. *Carpe diem*—"seize the day"—is an existential philosophy. "You only go around once in life, so grab all the gusto you can" is an existential philosophy.

Among the many problems with existentialism is this one pointed out by the late philosopher and theologian Francis Schaeffer: what is one man's existential pleasure is another's existential pain. The committed existentialist sitting on a park bench becomes far less committed to existentialism—experience as a measure of truth—when a robber relieves him of his wallet. When experience impacts us negatively, existentialism has less to commend it.

The third *-ism* is *relativism*, the one that probably affects us most. With relativism, truth becomes a moving target—everything is relative to everything else. Individuals set their own standards in life just like they did in the days of the Old Testament judges when everyone did what was right in their own eyes (Judg. 17:6; 21:25). The classic example of relativism among Christians is when we think that "at least I'm not as bad as So-and-so." Well, So-and-so is not the standard—Christ is. And yet we continue to be deceived into thinking that God grades on the curve like our eighth-grade algebra teacher did. That is deception of the highest order.

Our fleshly, human nature soaks up *-isms* like a blotter soaking up water because they make us feel good and smart. But they are foolishness in God's sight and a ready reference for the deceptive work of God's enemy and ours.

The Domain of Materialism

By the time king Solomon reached his sunset years, he was a more realistic, if not cynical, man. He wrote the Song of Solomon in his idyllic youth, Proverbs in his practical years of rule, and Ecclesiastes in his twilight years after discovering that life holds little in the way of meaning. While drifting away from God, marrying hundreds of foreign wives, and incorporating their worship into Israel's, he set out to discover life in its fullness—and he found nothing. He learned that life lived apart from God is vain and meaningless.

One of the avenues Solomon pursued was wealth and all it could buy. Would he find in materialism the answers he looked for? His own words tell the tale: "He who loves silver will not be satisfied with silver; nor he who loves abundance, with increase. This also is vanity" (Eccles. 5:10). Solomon discovered that money alone is deceptively captivating but ultimately disappointing apart from the eternal purposes of God.

Another searcher, centuries later, echoed the same sentiment. H. G. Wells said, "Money—money, like everything else—is a deception and a disappointment."

Jesus spoke of the deceitfulness of riches in the parable of the sower (Mark 4:19): "The cares of this world, the deceitfulness of riches, and the desires for other things" are enough to "choke the word, and it becomes unfruitful." All three of these interlopers are related—they all have to do with materialism, the lust for the things of this world. In our day and in our culture, this may be the most powerful *-ism* combating the health and holiness of the church. We have become cultural Christians instead of committed Christians, too comfortable in the affluence with which we have been blessed. If the church doesn't see this reality and denies that it exists, is it because we are deceived? Remember: *a deceived person doesn't know he's deceived.* Are we in the middle of spiritual warfare without realizing it?

Saint Augustine wrote in *The City of God*,

> Let us imagine two individuals. Of these two men, let us suppose that one is poor, or better, in moderate circumstances; the other, extremely wealthy. But, our wealthy man is haunted by fear, heavy with cares, feverish with greed, never secure, always restless, breathless from endless quarrels with his enemies. By these miseries, he adds to his possessions beyond measure, but he also piles up for himself a mountain of distressing worries. The man of modest means is content with a small and compact patrimony. He is loved by his own, enjoys the sweetness of peace in his relations with kindred, neighbors, and friends, is religious and pious, of kindly disposition, healthy in body, self-restrained, chaste in morals, and at peace with his conscience. I wonder if there is anyone so senseless as to hesitate over which of the two to prefer. What is true of these two individuals is likewise true of two families, two nations, two kingdoms; the analogy holds in both cases.[1]

Do you hesitate over which of the two to prefer? If so, be careful: the battle lines of spiritual warfare are being drawn.

The Domain of Counterfeits

For years preachers loved to use the illustration about how the Treasury Department taught its agents to detect counterfeit money by studying the real thing instead of counterfeits. While that has since been established as an urban legend, it still makes sense—and even more so in the spiritual realm. Our world is full of counterfeit sources of peace, happiness, joy, success, and true wealth. We live in a spiritual age not unlike the days of the gold rush when neophyte prospectors would hit a vein of pyrite, fool's gold, and think they had struck it rich because it looked similar to the real thing.

The god of this world, Satan, is a master counterfeiter. The apostle Paul tells us that "Satan himself transforms himself into an angel of light. Therefore it is no great thing if his ministers also transform themselves into ministers of righteousness, whose end will be according to their works" (2 Cor. 11:14–15). Not only is Satan a deceiver; he empowers his agents in this world to masquerade as truth speakers ("false apostles," v. 13). In fact, it is highly likely that it was one of those deceiving messengers of Satan that Paul refers to as the "thorn" in his flesh in the very next chapter of 2 Corinthians (12:7).

If "the whole world lies under the sway of the wicked one" (1 John 5:19) and he is a master of counterfeiting, then we must learn to be suspect of almost everything we encounter in this world. I'm not talking about producing paranoia so we're afraid to leave the house for fear of mistaking who or what to trust. I'm talking about walking so closely with the Spirit of God and being so steeped in the values of the kingdom of God that when we run across the equivalent of pyrite in our daily travels, we are not consumed with lust and sell our soul to gain it. If we do, we become the fools that Solomon warned against in Proverbs 2, enticed by the siren songs of this world's counterfeits.

The relentless, persistent, never-ending acquisition of wisdom, interpreted and applied by the Holy Spirit, is the only way I know to grow in the ability to discern counterfeits of Satan from the reality of God in life. We are not smarter than Satan, regardless of what we think. He can set traps for us today that have implications months, even years, down the road. We think we can live right up next to the line separating truth from error and be safe. But what if the line itself is a counterfeit? That's why Paul says to "flee" so often: flee sexual immorality (1 Cor. 6:18), flee idolatry (1 Cor. 10:14), flee carnal behavior (1 Tim. 6:11), and flee youthful lusts (2 Tim. 2:22). He doesn't say "walk next to them but don't cross the line!" We're not smart enough to tell the real line from a counterfeit. Better to flee in the opposite direction to make sure we're nowhere near the line that can send us to destruction.

On the flip side, James says the devil will flee from us if we are submitted to God (James 4:7). Since a deceived person doesn't know he's deceived, the only way to ensure you're not is to stay fully submitted to God, moment by moment, day by day, all your life long.

Discussion Questions

1. What does it mean to you to know that your heart is "deceitful above all things?" How do you know when to trust your heart and when not to trust it?

2. If it's true that a deceived person doesn't know when he is deceived, how important is the Holy Spirit's role in safeguarding against deception? How do you personally make yourself available to the Spirit for His role as Counselor?

3. Which of the four *-isms* mentioned in the chapter—humanism, existentialism, relativism, materialism—are most attractive to you? Against which do you have to guard your heart most diligently?

4. What part of materialism is most attractive to you—financial security, pleasure, status? How do you guard against the deceitfulness of materialism in your life?

5. What is the best way you have found to guard against counterfeit reality in your life and in the world? What spiritual disciplines do you most depend on to maintain spiritual clarity?

1. Saint Augustine, *The City of God* (New York: Penguin Books; reprint edition, 2003).

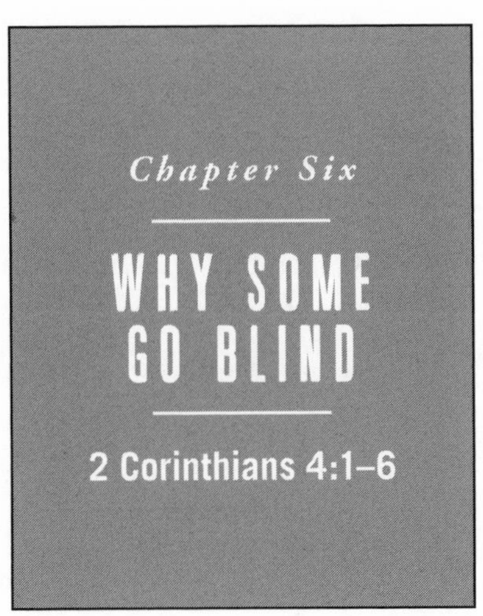

Chapter Six

WHY SOME GO BLIND

2 Corinthians 4:1–6

THE OCTOBER 1993 ISSUE of *Life* magazine introduced a term to the world that had not been widely known: *organ nappers.* And the article sent chills of horror down the spines of civilized people.

The story was about a ten-year-old Colombian boy named Jensen, pictured in the article playing a flute. It took a second look at the picture to imagine the kinds of sad songs he must have grown up playing. For one look at his sad eyes—or at least where his eyes should have been—showed only grotesque, empty sockets. Jensen lived in a charitable institution in Bogotá, Columbia, and was a victim of organ nappers—eye thieves—when he was only ten months old.

Jensen's mother had taken him to the hospital because of his acute diarrhea. She had to leave him overnight, and when she returned the next day, she found his eyes covered with bloody bandages and dried blood spattered on his body and bed. Incredulous and horrified at the same time, she demanded to know what had happened to her son. A doctor answered her harshly, "Can't you see your child is dying?" and disappeared.

Jensen's mother rescued him from the hospital and rushed him to another medical facility in Bogotá. The doctor who examined him there gave her the unbelievable news: "They've stolen his eyes." Thieves had cut the child's eyeballs out of his head to sell on the human organ black market. Jensen was fortunate to have even lived. Organ traffickers in Colombia usually just killed their victims, removed the organs, and sold them to the highest bidder—in Jensen's case, someone needing cornea transplants.

Jensen would never see his mother's face again and never see other children or the beauty of nature. For the rest of his life, he will live in a world of darkness.

As horrible as Jensen's fate is, there is another kind of blindness that has implications far beyond losing one's physical sight: losing one's spiritual sight. Imagine being blinded spiritually so your heart remained in darkness not only in time but for all eternity. Physical blindness only has temporary ramifications, but spiritual blindness has results that echo far beyond the grave.

The spiritual organ napper is Satan. He is out to steal the spiritual eyes of anyone he can to prevent them from seeing their sin and beholding the grace of God. Satan's mission to steal the spiritual eyes of human beings is the reason some people go spiritually blind and never find their way to the Savior. Some sit in church and yawn while others sit on the edge of their pew and drink in every word.

Paul talked about the blinding work of Satan: "But even if our gospel is veiled, it is veiled to those who are perishing, *whose minds the god of this age has blinded*, who do not believe, lest the light of the gospel of the glory of Christ, who is the image of God, should shine on them" (2 Cor. 4:3–4, italics mine). Paul goes on to say in verse 6 that God commands light to shine into the darkness of the human heart to give the knowledge of the glory of God. But if Satan has snatched away the eyes of the heart—if a person is in spiritual blindness—he will never see that light.

What is Satan so scared that man might see? The truth about God, of course. If he can blind the eyes of the unbelieving, and even hamper the spiritual eyesight of believers, he keeps them from seeing the glory of God and living in light of it. One of the ways Satan blinds human eyes is by distorting God and His character. If you think you see God clearly but are looking at a caricature of Him, you might as well be blind. Not to see God as He truly is gains no advantage over not seeing Him at all.

Warning: Blindness Ahead

Consider two instructions to keep you out of this potential deadly round of spiritual warfare.

1. Be on your guard. Paul gives the first warning in Ephesians 4:27: "Do not give the devil a foothold" (NIV). Don't let the devil get his foot in the door of your heart.

Paul issued this exhortation in the context of a warning about sinful anger, but it holds for any kind of sinful behavior. Any time we willingly choose to walk in the flesh instead of the Spirit, we are issuing an engraved invitation to the devil to commence his attack on us. Who would think that a slight, willful sin could open the door to spiritual blindness down the road? But it most definitely can. Think of the heroin addict who thought experimenting with cigarettes in high school couldn't do any harm. With every sin we willingly commit and fail to repent of, more of Satan's hand goes over the eyes of our heart. Pretty soon we can't see truth at all.

2. Don't let evil be turned to good. An inverse correlation exists between what God says and what Satan says. If God says something is good, Satan wants to make it appear as evil. And if God says something is evil, Satan wants to make it appear to be good. When Satan or his representatives try to convince you that something evil is good, you are on the verge of entering into spiritual blindness. The devil's native language is lies (John 8:44). Nothing he ever says to you will be the truth or be said for reasons that are truthful. (More on this below.)

I can summarize these two warnings in a verse I cited in a previous chapter, Proverbs 4:23: "Keep your heart with all diligence, for out of it spring the issues of life." In matters of war, forewarned is forearmed.

Now let's focus on the ways Satan tries to blind us, using his means of establishing a foothold and contradicting what God says about what is good and what is evil.

The Blinding Tactics of Satan

In 1995 *Jane's International Defense Review* published a startling report on a new Chinese weapon: a portable offensive battlefield laser "disturber," the ZM-87. Its purpose is to blind or "dizzy" the eyes of enemy soldiers using high-powered laser pulses. It was targeted at "especially anybody who is sighting and firing . . . [by means of] an optical instrument, so as to cause him to lose combat ability or result in suppression of his observation and sighting operation." The weapon has a "flashblinding and damage range" of up to 10 kilometers, depending on weather conditions.

What good is a soldier in battle who can't see or can't focus on a target? In warfare, whether physical or spiritual, the ability to see clearly is critical.

Satan Blinds Us to God's Power

On Wednesday, October 11, 1994, NASA flight engineers sent the Magellan space explorer plummeting toward the planet Venus. It burned up in the atmosphere before ever reaching the surface. The craft had circled Venus more than fifteen thousand times since reaching its destination in 1990, so why did they intentionally destroy the $900 million spacecraft? It was out of power. Magellan's batteries were so spent that it could no longer transmit data to earth, which meant it was useless.

There's a parallel there for us: without God's power, we are useless in matters of the kingdom. For that reason, Satan does whatever he can to blind us to the power of God and make us see only our own fleshly strength. Whether subtly telling us that "God helps those who help themselves" or convincing us God isn't willing to help—either way, we are blind to the truth: it is only God's power that can quicken and equip the Christian to live a fruitful life.

Paul was often criticized for his human frailty and weaknesses and for the suffering he endured as an apostle. In 2 Corinthians 4:7 he corrected the perspective of those critics who misunderstood the nature of the Christian life: "But we have this treasure [of the gospel] in earthen vessels, that the excellence of the power may be of God and not of us." Paul was saying, "You're right—I have no power! God uses frail human beings to demonstrate *His* power, not *ours.*" Isn't that why he wrote in Galatians 2:20, "It is no longer I who live, but Christ lives in me"? And in 2 Corinthians 12:9, "Therefore most gladly I will rather boast in my infirmities, that the power of Christ may rest upon me"? Though we may be confused or blinded to the truth of where power originates for the Christian life, Paul was not.

I have talked to more than one non-Christian through the years whose objection to entering into a relationship with Christ went like this: "Oh, I could never be a Christian—I'm not strong enough. I'd never be able to keep up with my end of the bargain." That's the "God helps those who help themselves" deal again. What non-Christians don't understand is that the Christian life is not difficult, it's impossible. The power for living a victorious life comes from God, not from us.

While I can understand non-Christians being confused about the issue of power, I'm less understanding when I find Christians blinded to the same truth: "I don't have the courage to go witnessing. . . . I'm too scared to sing that solo in front of the church. . . . I don't have the energy to get to that 6:00 a.m. Bible study. . . . I'm too old to go on that missions trip."

Christians forget that we live the Christian life the same way we entered it—totally by the power of God. It is "Christ in you" that is your "hope of glory" (Col 1:27), not "you in you."

Satan Blinds Us to God's Holiness

Consider this fable: As an infant, a child is kidnapped by a malevolent person and raised in an environment where he is taught the opposite of everything that is true in the real world. He is taught that up is down, black is white, lies are good, and serving self is the highest priority. Then, when the child is rescued from his evil captor as a young adult and reintroduced to normal life, he finds that he has to relearn everything: up is up, black is black, lies are bad, and serving others is the highest priority.

One of the principal things he has to learn—and that we have to learn as new residents of the kingdom of God—is that God, and everything He touches, is holy. We're like Moses when he was standing in front of the burning bush on the mountain of God. Moses learned that even dirt was holy if it was being used in the service of God: "Take your sandals off your feet, for the place where you stand is holy ground" (Exod. 3:5). In Leviticus we learn that tents, pots and pans, knives—everything used in the worship of God—are holy and are therefore to be treated with reverence and respect.

The whole idea of "holy" is to be set apart. So if God sets something—or someone—apart for a special purpose, that thing or person is made holy by its "set-apartness." It is no longer common or profane, but holy. That's why Christians are called *saints* ("holy ones") in the New Testament—because we have been called by God into His service.

Satan would have us believe that things in this life are not holy and therefore are not to be treated with the same reverence with which we treat God. The world has no motivation for calling anything holy—not their bodies, creation, marriage, sex, jobs, recreation, money. It's all just "stuff" to the world.

But for the Christian, everything about us and our lives is holy since it all belongs to God. Our relationships and possessions; our physical, mental, and emotional beings—all are His and therefore all holy. The sacred/secular dichotomy that the world talks about is a false paradigm for the Christian. It's *all* sacred. We reveal that we live by that false dichotomy when we take our Bibles to church on Sunday (the Lord's day) and don't touch them Monday through Saturday (our days).

The great spiritual battle that is taking place in our culture is Satan trying to turn everything good into evil, while God is trying to turn everything evil into good. God's Word through Isaiah still applies today: "Woe to those who call evil good, and good evil; who put darkness for light, and light for darkness; who put bitter for sweet, and sweet for bitter!" (Isa. 5:20). When churches sanction homosexuality, abortion, the dissolution of marriages for trivial reasons, and other cultural practices, they are demonstrating their spiritual blindness. They have called what is evil good. And woe to them.

Satan Blinds Us to God's Wisdom

The next time you're in a large bookstore, spend some time perusing the "self-help" section. There you'll find books on what we would refer to as "counseling issues"—lifestyle matters dealing with mental and emotional maturity, relationships, finances, spirituality, child-rearing, and other issues. The books look inviting, and no doubt many of them contain some nuggets of truth and wisdom. But regardless of their potential benefit, if they are offering wisdom from a nonbiblical perspective, you ought to see a red flag attached to the spine of each one.

Why? Because the psalmist wrote, "Blessed is the man who walks not in the counsel of the ungodly" (Ps. 1:1). Does that mean you can't accept wisdom, advice, or counsel from anyone who isn't a Christian? Does the guy who works on your car have to be a Christian to give you guidance about making it run better and last longer? Of course not.

But Satan would have us believe that "all advice is God's advice"—that "in the great scope of the cosmic drama in which we play a part we shouldn't fear receiving wisdom from any well-intentioned and self-anointed expert." That's exactly where spiritual blindness sets in—when we start believing truth can be found anywhere.

Paul explains why this isn't true in 1 Corinthians 2:9—"Eye has not seen, nor ear heard, nor have entered into the heart of man the things which God has prepared for those who love Him." In other words, the natural senses of man are not able to receive the things of God. The wisdom of God is "hidden wisdom" (v. 7), not known by the world. If they don't know it, they don't have it. And if they don't have it, they can't dispense it. That's why we must be careful from whom we receive counsel and on what subject.

I never encourage Christians to "seek counsel," but to "seek *godly* counsel." The wisdom of God is revealed by the Spirit of God who "searches all things, yes, the deep things of God" (1 Cor. 2:10). Paul concludes by saying that "the natural man does not receive the things of the Spirit of God, for they are foolishness to him; nor can he know them, because they are spiritually discerned" (v. 14).

When you seek counsel from some source, take it to heart, and begin to feel a check in your spirit about it—that's the Holy Spirit sounding a battle cry. The battle lines for spiritual warfare are forming as Satan attempts to blind the eyes of your heart to the true wisdom of God. In such cases, beating a hasty retreat is the better part of wisdom—and valor.

Satan Blinds Us to God's Justice

If you've ever planted anything—grass seed, tomatoes, flowers—you know there are two factors that are inviolable: time and kind. First, there is a time factor involved between planting and harvesting. Second, you will reap the same kind of harvest as the seed you planted. Take the radish, for example. It's the fastest to germinate and bear in the vegetable garden, but it still takes two to three weeks to get a radish for your salad. And you will get a radish—not a bean, tomato, or squash.

The laws of the harvest that God has built into the botanical part of His creation—the laws of time and kind—carry over to the spiritual realm as well. Paul says plainly in Galatians 6:7, "Do not be deceived, God is not mocked; for whatever a man sows, that he will also reap." You *will* reap (a function of time), and you will reap consistent with what you sow (a function of kind). The laws of the harvest are reflections and expressions of God's justice. Cause and effect are built into the economy of the rule of God, and justice is what governs the relationship between the two.

The danger for those living in the kingdom is to think that God's laws of harvest do not apply in the spiritual realm like they do in the botanical realm. Paul highlights that danger by warning, "Do not be deceived." It is primarily the function of time that is most deceptive. Because we don't automatically see the repercussions of our actions we deceive ourselves into thinking there won't be any. It's like a gardener who forgets he planted a seed and is then shocked when a plant appears. Satan will do everything he can to blind us to God's justice; to convince us that the laws of time and kind—God's law of spiritual harvest—do not apply to us. God is mocked—by Satan and by us—when we become blind to the laws of harvest; when we become blind toward God's sense of justice. Thus Paul's words, "God is not mocked."

Those words contain the ultimate warning: God is not and will not be mocked by us or by Satan. That means God's justice will prevail in every quarter to keep cause and effect in a steady state of equilibrium in this world.

Because of the function of time (what appear to be delays between causes and effects), we are tempted to think God's justice is on temporary leave. For instance, I read recently of a person who had racked up a $150,000 balance on his credit cards but hadn't made a payment in over a year. I compare that with my own experience: the few times I have ever mailed a payment in that arrived past the due date, you would have thought I had tried to breach the gates of Fort Knox and steal the nation's gold. Letters, phone calls, blots on my credit record—how could a slight error in paying my paltry balance get such a reaction when others spend freely with no apparent repercussions?

Because a day is like a thousand years to God (2 Pet. 3:8), time is not a function to Him. Everything—past, present, and future—exists in the eternal "now." There is no difference between a year's overdue payment of one person and my two-day overdue payment. His justice is at work within the mystery of His own will to balance all accounts according to His good pleasure.

Don't ignore God's justice as expressed in the laws of spiritual harvest. Don't think you can sow and not reap. If you do, you enter immediately into spiritual warfare in which Satan mocks God throughout the heavenly places by your actions on earth. And in the end, because God will not be mocked, you will reap what you have sown.

Satan Blinds Us to God's Grace

In 1994, Marcio de Silva, a Brazilian artist, was so distraught over his girlfriend's ending their relationship that he tried to win her back with works of devotion. He decided to walk to her house on his knees, a distance of nine miles, to prove his love for her. With pieces of rubber tires tied to his knees, he shuffled along for fourteen hours before reaching her home. His nineteen-year-old girlfriend was not impressed—she had heard of his strategy and left home before he arrived.

Love is a gift that cannot be earned. In fact, it is given in spite of being wholly undeserved. Paul tells us that the love of God, revealed by grace leading to faith, is a pure gift of God (Eph. 2:8–9). Given what we know of Satan, we should not be surprised to find him blinding our eyes to the grace of God and convincing us that we must work to obtain His favor. When we try to approach God and relate to Him on the basis of works, we have entered the realm of spiritual warfare. In his efforts to mischaracterize God, Satan will make every effort to discredit His grace: "So you're a God of grace. Look at Corts down there on earth, sweating and agonizing, trying to earn Your forgiveness for that sin he just committed."

I confess to having fallen into the "works" trap at times, blinded to the grace of God. And then when I reach a place of mental and spiritual exhaustion—which usually doesn't take long—I remember: for by grace I am saved, not by works, lest I should boast.

All I have to do to correct that mind-set is to reread Hebrews 11, God's Hall of Faith, where the word *faith* occurs twenty-four times. If I read through that chapter substituting the word *works* for *faith,* it becomes almost laughable: "by *works* Abel . . . by works Enoch . . . by works Noah . . . by *works* Abraham . . . by works Sarah . . . these all died in [their] *works* . . . by works Isaac . . . by works Jacob . . . by works Joseph . . . by works the harlot Rahab . . . and all these, having obtained a good testimony through works, did not receive the promise." The idea that any of these saints could have accomplished what they did by sheer grit and willpower is absurd. They were Hall of Famers, but not because of their works. They were fallible men and women whose sins, in spite of their good works, would have kept them far from the gates of heaven without the grace of God.

Far better to be like the apostle Paul, who went from being blinded *to* the grace of God (Phil. 3:4–6) to being blinded *by* the grace of God (Acts 9:1–19, especially v. 18). Whatever it is you think God couldn't possibly do for you because of your failures and sins . . . you're right! But God will do it for you because of His grace in Jesus Christ. Just as Satan was defeated the day Paul's eyes were opened to the grace of God, so can he be defeated in your life if you will throw off the blinders that prevent you from seeing His grace.

Be on your guard and don't let Satan turn what is evil into something that appears to be good. When you do, you go blind—blind to the power, holiness, wisdom, justice, and grace of God. Satan is an organ napper who will steal the eyes of your heart the moment you let down your guard. You haven't seen anything until you discover you can't see God. Far better to walk in the light while you have it.

Discussion Questions

1. To what degree do you believe Satan can influence a Christian? What are the evidences that demonic forces are influencing a Christian?

2. Name any activities or behaviors in which it is even remotely possible that Satan could gain a foothold in your life. What confidence do you have that he won't? How do you defend yourself?

3. Describe an area of your life in which you are having a hard time believing God for success or victory. To what degree might Satan be blinding you to the power of God?

4. To what extent does the sacred/secular dichotomy influence your life? What parts of your life, if any, do you have a hard time viewing as sacred?

5. Describe any area of your life in which you are sowing seeds for bad or useless fruit. To what degree do you doubt the underlying certainty of God's law of the harvest?

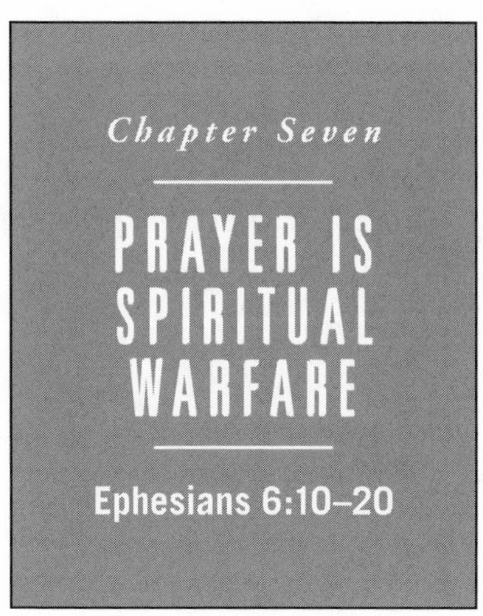

Chapter Seven

PRAYER IS SPIRITUAL WARFARE

Ephesians 6:10–20

FOR MANY YEARS Israeli Defense Forces recruits were taken to the top of a high mountain in Israel where they would shout out, "Masada will never fall again!" But it was not just any mountain where they stood with torches burning in the night—it was Masada itself, the legendary Jewish stronghold.

Masada is perhaps the most famous military stronghold in the world. With the introduction of airplanes into military conflict in the modern era, the value of impregnable mountain fortresses fell like the stones they were built from. But in biblical days, everyone knew what a stronghold was—the last line of defense against an enemy. (Strongholds are mentioned nearly fifty times in the Bible.)

Masada was where, according to the Jewish historian Josephus, a company of nearly one thousand Jewish zealots held out against the armies of Rome in the first century. Jerusalem was sacked by the Roman general Titus in AD 70, and the company of Jews who sought refuge at Masada ("mountain fortress"), which

Herod had fortified as a palace-fortress years before, lasted until AD 73. Masada is Israel's most popular archaeological tourist stop today, and for good reason. Now reachable via cable car, Masada had only a circuitous access path snaking up the side of sheer cliffs in AD 73.

After failing to starve the Jews out, the Roman general Silva spent eight months building a three-hundred-foot-high stone siege ramp by which his soldiers eventually breached Masada's walls. But when they entered the stronghold, they discovered that the Jews, with the exception of two women and a few children, were all dead. They had committed suicide rather than be captured and killed or enslaved by the Romans.

It is easy to see why, in the early decades of Israel's modern existence, Israeli Defense Forces recruits were taken to the top of Masada to vow that it would never fall again. Only the Rock of Gibraltar at the entrance to the Mediterranean offers a better picture of stability, immovability, and permanence. That's what Masada represents to the Israeli army—and that's what a stronghold was for: to be a place that could not, and would not, be moved.

Varieties of Strongholds

It's important to remember that strongholds are amoral—anybody can build one and use it for his or her purposes. And while strongholds were originally physical, they can be mental, emotional, or spiritual as well. The apostle Paul, for instance, discovered that spiritual and mental strongholds had been erected in Corinth. There were false apostles in the church who were slandering him and attempting to ruin his reputation among the believers. In fact, much of his letter of 2 Corinthians is spent "pulling down strongholds" (2 Cor. 10:4) that had been built by the false teachers. He did not use carnal methods of retaliation against them but rather chose to "[cast] down arguments and every high thing that exalts itself against the knowledge of God, bringing every thought into captivity to the obedience of Christ" (v. 5).

The strongholds in Corinth had been constructed out of mountains of misinformation and were designed to keep out the truth about Paul and other godly apostles. And guess who was behind the construction of the strongholds: Satan. It was his servants, the false apostles, who were masquerading as "ministers of righteousness" in Corinth (2 Cor. 11:13–15).

Satan is still constructing strongholds today in the minds of people everywhere—even Christians. His purpose? To keep the truth about God from those who need to know Him and learn to trust Him. All spiritual warfare begins in heaven as attacks on God by Satan. It then spills over onto earth as Satan uses deception and lies to build up mental and emotional strongholds in the minds of people against God.

And this is not a theoretical battle. Paul, in Ephesians 6, outlines the armor that every Christian must wear daily to withstand the attacks of the enemy: truth, the gospel, faith, salvation, the Word of God, and prayer (vv. 14–18). It is this last weapon, prayer, that is so critical in spiritual warfare. Prayer takes us into the heavenly places, before the throne of God to ask for resources and resolve to break through the strongholds that Satan is erecting.

How Strongholds Are Built

We can almost tell which of the weapons of our spiritual warfare are the most critical by looking at the one we use the least. For most Christians, that would be prayer. We would rather read our Bible, believe God, have faith, share the gospel—anything but pray "with all perseverance and supplication for all the saints" (Eph. 6:18). The church's weapons are not stained glass, padded pews, shiny buses, or sparkling facilities. None of those will defeat the devil. But prayer will. Praying the truth of God and standing on the promises of God in prayer will breach any and every stronghold that Satan can build.

How does Satan build the strongholds that keep us from accomplishing the will of God in this world? He does it in the same way Masada was fortified—taking individual stones and stacking them repetitively until a fortress wall was completed.

In the same way, a spiritual stronghold is erected with a single idea spoken enough times until it takes on the appearance of reality.

I remember seeing a tough law enforcement officer who attended our church working in the nursery with the babies. On the exterior, this was a take-charge individual who would brook no dissent and display no tenderness in his job. He was a police captain—he was paid to maintain a law-and-order persona, and that is how I thought of him. I had built up a stronghold about this man in my mind such that I would never have imagined he would be suitable for working in a nursery with little babies. But when I walked by the nursery door and saw him rocking an infant and cooing tenderly to it . . . well, my stronghold was completely demolished. I saw a totally different side of this man that I had never seen before.

I was wrong to have built up a one-sided impression of him based on limited exposure. Without even knowing it, I had established a stronghold, one brick-like thought at a time, until I thought a certain way. And that's exactly how we learn to think about anything or anybody—God included. That's why it is so important to take every thought captive to the Word and will of Christ. How would Jesus think about this subject or this person? If we are not careful, our thoughts and experiences will construct a stronghold about God Himself.

And that's where Satan comes in. Just like he used his false apostles to get the Corinthian church to think wrongly about the apostle Paul, so he uses every method he can to get us to think wrongly about God. His ultimate purpose in building defenses against the truth of God? To thwart our prayers. If you don't believe God is sovereign, responsive, communicative, safe, and strong, why would you pray to Him?

But I believe those things about God, you object. Do you really? Our prayer life is a direct reflection of what we believe—*really* believe—about God. What if your lack of prayer proves that you have an entirely different stronghold of thought about God—one that doesn't view Him as sovereign, responsive, communicative, safe, and strong?

In biblical days, strongholds were often built by capitalizing on a natural formation—a cliff, cave, or promontory of some sort. Defensive enhancements were added in a way that blended in the natural surroundings. Standing at the base of Masada, for instance, it would have been nearly impossible to tell what intricate defensive measures had been established on top. In the same way that strongholds blend into the environment, so lies about God can blend into our spiritual environment if we are not careful.

It's the difference between *thinking* that God is sovereign, responsive, communicative, safe, and strong, and *believing* that He is.

Satan's Five Strongholds against Believers' Prayers

Satan attempts to erect the following five strongholds to thwart your prayer life. Why? Because of what the poet William Cowper put so beautifully: "And Satan trembles when he sees the weakest saint upon his knees."

Stronghold One: God Is Not Sovereign

The question your children ask you is the very same question Satan loves to tempt us to ask God: *why*? Not that there's anything wrong with asking God when it's done with a spirit of submission. But Satan likes to build up the idea that God isn't any more in control of life than we are. After all, if He is in control, when you ask Him *why,* wouldn't He tell you? The very fact that He doesn't answer means He can't be trusted and isn't really sovereign.

Daniel is a book in the Bible where the sovereignty of God is showcased. In Daniel 2, Daniel interprets a dream for the king of Babylon, saying, "Blessed be the name of God forever and ever, for wisdom and might are His. And He changes the times and the seasons; He removes kings and raises up kings; He gives wisdom to the wise and knowledge to those who have understanding. He reveals deep and secret things; He knows what is in the darkness, and light dwells with Him" (vv. 20–22).

Nebuchadnezzar himself had a life-changing encounter with God and declared that "[God's] dominion is an everlasting dominion, and His kingdom is from generation to generation.

All the inhabitants of the earth are reputed as nothing; He does according to His will in the army of heaven and among the inhabitants of the earth. No one can restrain His hand or say to Him, 'What have You done?'" (Dan. 4:34–35).

These great statements of praise are culled from the experiences of life. They paint a picture of a God who is in charge of the world He created, who acts according to His own purposes and plans.

Did you hear of the young woman who brought her fiancé home to meet her parents? After dinner, the girl's father and the young man retired to the study, where the father inquired about the young man's future plans and ability to provide for his daughter. The young man declared that he was a Bible scholar, to which the father responded, "But how will you buy an engagement ring . . . buy a house and car . . . support children . . . provide for a family?"

To each of these questions, the idealistic young man answered, "I will pursue my studies and God will provide."

Later the mother asked the father how the conversation went. "Well," he said, "the young man has no job and no plans, but the good news is he thinks I'm God!"

Unfortunately that's where many Christians end up when they encounter Satan's stronghold against God's sovereignty: they think it's up to them to play God. They think that, even if God is sovereign, His sovereignty doesn't extend down to the practical matters of life like money, family, and daily bread. So why pray if God isn't going to get involved in the details of life? Thankfully, the Bible is filled with examples of this stronghold being full of chinks. For example, Jesus taught His disciples to pray, "Give us this day our daily bread" (Matt. 6:11).

Stronghold Two: God Is Slow

When I read in the biography of George Muller that he prayed for sixty years for the salvation of two friends, I examined my own perceptions about God to see if I had allowed a stronghold to be built. Several days before Muller died, one of the friends was saved and several days after he died the other was saved. Regarding the second one, whom Muller did not have the joy of seeing come to Christ, I thought of Abraham who "died in faith, not having received the promises, but having seen them afar off [was] assured of them" (Heb. 11:13).

While Abraham is a good example overall of not losing faith because he didn't see everything God promised, he is also a good example of why we get defeated by this stronghold—because we have an undisciplined spirit. God had promised Abraham a son, but he and Sarah remained childless into their old age. Because God's schedule wasn't the same as Abraham's, the great man of faith lay with Sarah's handmaid, Hagar, and bore a son through her—Ishmael (Gen. 16). This son of Abraham bore descendants (Arabs) who remain a thorn in the side of Israel to this day. Abraham's impatience brought forth the modern Arab-Israeli conflict that has colored the sands of Palestine red with the blood of the slain.

The Bible makes a very clear statement regarding the speed with which God does things: "Don't overlook the obvious here, friends. With God, one day is as good as a thousand years, a thousand years as a day. God isn't late with His promise as some measure lateness" (2 Pet. 3:8–9 *The Message*). In other words, God is not bound by time as we are. All of eternity appears before God as a single picture—completed, finished, orchestrated perfectly.

If you crash into the stronghold that God is slow and therefore cannot be trusted, you will stop praying for anything. Someday in heaven you will hear George Muller's friends thanking him that he tore down that stronghold and prayed through to their salvation. Muller knew that "the Lord is not slow in keeping his promise, as some understand slowness. He is patient with you, not wanting anyone to perish, but everyone to come to repentance" (2 Pet. 3:9 NIV).

Stronghold Three: God Is Silent

If you are in a noisy room, listening to two people talk, your brain can distinguish and track the voice of either of the two. Add a third person and the brain can still usually isolate and focus in on one voice. But if a thousand people are talking at once in an auditorium, your brain is overloaded with frequencies—it can't pick out any one voice to track. That's the principle behind the popular white-noise generators used by people today in offices and bedrooms—anywhere extraneous noises need to be silenced. The noise devices overload the brain with numerous frequencies—none of which are very loud—thereby making it impossible to focus on extraneous noises.

I'm convinced that a lot of people who think God is silent—"I never sense God speaking or communicating to me"—are suffering from white-noise overload. We are so inundated with the noise of our culture that it cancels out the still, small voice of God. It's not that God is silent; it's that we can't hear because our ears are filled with so much other noise. The white noises come from many cultural devices such as television, newspapers, and social and cultural busyness. God is speaking but we cannot hear. In the Christian life we counter the white noise which prevents us from hearing God through reading the Word, maintaining a quiet time, meditating on the character of God, and conversing with Him in prayer. As we turn our hearts and minds toward the Lord, we overcome the cultural noise which prevents our hearing the voice of God.

On the other hand, God is not an incessant talker. He speaks only when He has something to say that we need to hear (witness the four hundred years between the Old and New Testaments during which God was silent). But when God doesn't speak, we think it's because He can't speak—that He lacks wisdom about the situation we're in—and a stronghold develops in our mind.

In the first century of the church Christians often extended a greeting to one another by saying, "Maranatha!" ("O Lord, come!" 1 Cor. 16:22). After several generations, when it appeared the Lord was silent and was not coming, they stopped using the greeting. A stronghold had developed because they didn't submit their expectations to the Lord's timetable. They failed to see that the Lord was delaying His return because He was "not willing that any should perish but that all should come to repentance" (2 Pet. 3:9).

When John the Baptist was in jail, he sent a message to Jesus, asking if He was really the Messiah (Matt. 11:2–6). Jesus replied with a message that enumerated all the things He was doing (the blind see, the lame walk, the dead are raised, etc.) and concluded with this statement: "And blessed is he who is not offended because of Me." People are offended when God doesn't act like they think He should; they develop strongholds and stop praying. It is far better to do away with the white noise in our lives so we can hear Him when He does speak.

Stronghold Four: God Is Not Secure

My greatest breakthrough in parenting came when I realized it's OK to be misunderstood by my children. Not that I wanted to be misunderstood. But I learned that my security as a parent does not come from whether my little ones understand my every decision and action. My security as a parent comes from my relationship with God, my love for my children and my wife, and the knowledge that I was doing the very best I could to raise my children in the nurture and admonition of the Lord.

That same insight was a breakthrough in my spiritual life as well: God is content in Himself whether I understand Him or not. He doesn't need my understanding, much less my approval, of His actions, words, and choices. God is willing to act out of the counsel of His own will and risk being misunderstood by us, His children.

We have gone completely overboard on the self-esteem and political correctness themes today. Parents are afraid to make decisions their children might disagree with and they spend every waking moment telling their children how wonderful they are. I have seen young parents so afraid that their children are going to grow up with an inferiority complex that they compliment every breath their little precious ones take. Their children can do no wrong—which is just so much psychobabble. And it becomes just so much "theo-babble" when we expect God to act the same way toward us.

God is under no obligation to explain His actions to anyone. When He allows, or causes, something unpleasant to happen, we expect to be hand-delivered an explanation. That's evidence of a stronghold. Satan has convinced you that God is your servant and owes you an explanation for everything He does. And when those explanations don't come, you stop praying because you're acting like a child who doesn't get his way, who thinks his parent will respond if he throws a tantrum.

Reread the account of Jesus dealing with Mary and Martha when their brother Lazarus died (John 11). When He got word that Lazarus died, He delayed making His "pastoral visit" for two days (v. 6). The average pastor would be fired for doing that today. But Jesus never apologized or offered an explanation. He went about doing the will of the Father regardless of whom it might offend.

If you have grown confused about who is in charge in this world, I encourage you to begin tearing down that stronghold. Otherwise you'll be AWOL in spiritual warfare because the Commander-in-Chief didn't respond to your every request.

Stronghold Five: God Is Not Strong

Everyone knows the story of Jesus calming the winds when He and the disciples were crossing the Sea of Galilee. When they thought they were about to perish, the disciples asked Jesus, "Teacher, do You not care that we are perishing?" (Mark 4:38)—a perfect example of what has become a stronghold for many regarding God's strength.

When critics of the Bible address the question of suffering, they set God's caring against His strength. Either God cares when we are hurting but is not strong enough to help us, they say, or God is strong enough to help us but doesn't care enough. The disciples' question—"do You not care that we are perishing?"—implies they thought the latter.

Critics of God will not concede a third possibility: God is both strong enough and caring enough to help when we are hurting, but His purposes may not call for Him to intervene at the time we think He should.

Satan will work to convince us that God is not strong enough to meet our needs. *Oh, yes,* Satan whispers, *God may be loving to a degree, but His strength is not directed toward personal issues like you and I may have.* When we think that way, we give evidence of a stronghold concerning God's strength. Maybe it developed when you called on God for help and no help came—at least in the time and way you asked for. Maybe you resented God for not responding like you think a loving Father should.

Sometimes people react the opposite way to God's strength: they see His mighty power and are scared by it—overwhelmed to the point of intimidation. The disciples "feared exceedingly" (Mark 4:41) when they saw Jesus' power over the wind. And those who witnessed Jesus driving a legion of demons out of a man into a herd of swine begged Him to leave the area (Mark 5:17). They weren't comfortable in the presence of that kind of power.

If you have stopped praying for God to exercise His strength because you don't think He has any or you think He has too much, you've fallen victim to a stronghold of Satan.

How to Demolish Strongholds

To pull down strongholds and gain victory in spiritual warfare through prayer, you must take the following five steps.

1. Accept your position in Christ. If you are a Christian, here's what is true: you have been raised from spiritual death and are seated in the heavenly places in Christ (Eph. 2:6). You are a citizen of heaven, not of earth, and there are no strongholds against you in heaven. Therefore, you must bring your earthly experience in line with your heavenly position.

2. Assume your identity. When Jesus sent the seventy disciples out to minister in His name, they came back amazed at what they saw happen. They couldn't believe that demonic powers were subject to them in Jesus' name (Luke 10:17). You will be amazed too when you discover that, in Christ, you have power to tear down Satan's strongholds.

3. Acknowledge your authority. Jesus gave those seventy disciples "authority . . . over all the power of the enemy" (Luke 10:19). All authority has been given to Christ (Matt. 28:18) and, in Him, we have the right to exercise that authority against all the strongholds of the enemy.

4. Assure your purity. You cannot exercise authority against the devil if you have yielded a foothold to the devil in your life (Eph. 4:27). You cannot win a spiritual victory over Satan if he has won a moral victory over you.

5. Apply your authority. Spiritual warfare by prayer is spiritual labor—Jesus called it binding the strong man in order to plunder his house (Matt. 12:29). God does the binding, not us. But in the authority of Christ we pull down strongholds in prayer until we are free from the spiritual bondage that has blocked our victory in Christ. Authority is meaningless unless you exercise it.

When John Ashcroft was waiting to be sworn in as the new attorney general of the United States, his elderly father was nearby with the Ashcroft family. When they decided to pray together, and the elder Ashcroft attempted to get out of his chair, John Ashcroft told him he didn't need to stand up—it was fine if he remained seated. "I'm not struggling to stand, son," John's father said. "I'm struggling to get down on my knees."

On its knees is where the church will demolish the strongholds established against it—and where you will pull down those arrayed against you. Do not let a fortress that can be demolished keep you from claiming what is yours.

Discussion Questions

1. What strongholds are you aware of in your own life—traditions, beliefs, biases, prejudices? To what degree do they influence your walk with Christ in a negative way?

2. What should you do about strongholds you discover in your life? List three things to begin the process of demolishing strongholds in your life.

3. Practically speaking, how do you apply the spiritual armor that Paul describes in Ephesians 6? Is that literal or figurative language to you? Are they practical or theoretical instructions?

4. What level of frustration do you experience in attempting to hear the voice of God in your life? What correlation do you find between the amount of time you spend in silence with Him and your ability to hear His voice?

5. In light of this chapter, consider writing a version of 2 Corinthians 10:4–6 in your own words—an expanded, paraphrased version that reflects the practical realities of demolishing modern strongholds with spiritual weapons.

Chapter Eight

THE MORE, THE HOLIER

Mark 10:23–27

HE WAS HEAD OF A 2,300-ACRE THEME PARK that featured a Victorian-style hotel with a swimming pool in the lobby, a water park, campgrounds, and satellite television studios. He had one hundred fifty thousand paid partner-investors with annual salaries and bonuses running into the millions. He would spend $100,000 to have his clothes flown across country and $100 on cinnamon rolls to make his hotel room smell good. He had luxury mansions and condos in Palm Springs and other locales, a Rolls-Royce, and even air-conditioned dog kennels.

But the number that ultimately impressed Jim Bakker the most was 07407-058. That was the number assigned to him as a prison inmate when he began serving a forty-five-year prison sentence for mail fraud, investor fraud, and tax evasion.

By now probably most people know about the rise and fall of Jim and Tammy Faye Bakker and their PTL (Praise The Lord) televangelism empire. But it was not until Jim Bakker's release from prison and the publication of his book that we learned the rest of his story. In fact, I would not use Jim Bakker's experience as an example in this chapter had he not been so transparent about his own failures and repentance.

Before prison Jim Bakker believed, and taught others to believe, that it is God's will for every Christian to be rich; that wealth is a sign of God's blessing; that prosperity was a prelude to greatness in the kingdom of God. He told thousands of television viewers and visitors to the PTL empire that the more they gave to God, the more they would get from God; that God was obligated to bless them for their sacrificial giving. Prosperity and wealth were taught as the birthright of every believer.

After prison, the title of Jim Bakker's book said it all: *I Was Wrong*. He admitted that he had been wrong about what he believed and taught about money; that what he believed was not biblical; that he had been deceived into thinking that the more you have, the holier you are. Thank God for His grace that allowed Jim Bakker to see the error of his ways and publicly renounce them.

"The more, the holier." That's what I call this stronghold of Satan—the notion that the road to holiness is paved with riches. Far too many believers today use a sliding scale in evaluating their own adherence to the "the more, the holier" philosophy of life. They look at the extravagant wealth and lifestyles of the Bakkers (or others in our culture) and say, "Well, I'm certainly not that bad." Maybe not. But as I've said elsewhere in this book, no one in this world, Christian or otherwise, is the standard. The only thing that really matters is what God says through the living Word, Jesus Christ, or His written Word, the Bible.

In the last chapter I said that a stronghold is something that happens once, then gets repeated, and finally takes on the air of reality. A stronghold becomes a place to hide something or hide from someone. In his ongoing war against God, Satan has created a stronghold in the minds of many followers of Christ about wealth and prosperity. He seeks to convince us that wealth equals godliness so we will pursue riches as a means to attain righteousness. Then if we gain riches, we stand a good chance of getting entangled in them and forgetting about God. Or if we don't find riches, we become bitter toward God. Either way, Satan succeeds in using us as foils against God—his ultimate strategy in all spiritual warfare.

Jesus found that His own disciples were perplexed about the notion that, under the New Covenant, riches did not equal righteousness. In fact, we read in Mark 10:23–27 that they were "astonished" at Jesus' words, "How hard it is for those who have riches to enter the kingdom of God!" They replied, "Who then can be saved?"

Do you see the formula the disciples were working with? "We know that the richer you are, the more you are blessed by God. But if a rich man isn't blessed enough to make it to heaven, then who is?" They thought the godly were prosperous and the prosperous were godly. The Jewish leaders of Jesus' day, the Pharisees, were the most prosperous members of the society and set themselves forth as the most godly as well. And the disciples had bought into that worldview to the degree that it had become a stronghold in their minds. They couldn't imagine why it would be difficult for a rich man to enter the kingdom of God.

Caught in a Transition

Now, before I come down too hard on the disciples, let's clarify something about the context in which they made this statement. A massive transition was taking place between the Old and New Covenants. Jesus, obviously, was the hinge upon which the door from the Old to the New opened. The disciples shouldn't be faulted for what they didn't understand. (We don't have the same excuse.)

Under the Old Covenant, God promised Israel that, if they walked in His ways, they would be the most prosperous people on earth (Deut. 28:1–14). In fact, their prosperity would be evidence of God's blessing and would be a magnet to draw the nations to Himself (Zech. 8:23). Missiologists call this God's *centripetal* strategy: Israel was the center of God's presence on earth and His blessing would draw all nations to Himself. So for Israel, there was a cause-and-effect situation between riches and righteousness.

Sadly Israel failed to walk in God's ways and God withdrew His blessings as He had warned (Deut. 28:15–68). He made them a byword among the nations—slaves of Assyria and Babylon. When Jesus came not only to die for the sins of Israel but for the whole world, God's strategy changed from *centripetal* to *centrifugal.* Instead of drawing the nations to Jerusalem, He flung His people, the church, out from Jerusalem into the world to declare the gospel (Acts 1:8). No longer would riches be looked upon as evidence of God's blessings. Instead, the gift of righteousness would become the new evidence. To set the pattern for this change, Jesus sent groups of His disciples out, telling them, "Take nothing for the journey, neither staffs nor bag nor bread nor money; and do not have two tunics apiece" (Luke 9:3). And the greatest missionary-disciple of them all, the apostle Paul, said, "Having food and clothing, with these we shall be content" (1 Tim. 6:8).

In the Old Testament, the goal was for God's grace to be demonstrated in the physical world through the prosperity of the nation of Israel. In the New Testament, the goal is for God's grace to be demonstrated in the spiritual world through the spiritual power and humility of the church. We are exhorted to "lay aside every weight . . . [and] run with endurance the race that is set before us" (Heb. 12:1).

Can we excuse Jesus' disciples for not having instantly discerned the transition taking place when Jesus said how hard it was for a rich man to get to heaven? Of course. All of them eventually understood (except Judas), as evidenced by the sacrificial investment of their lives in the spread of the gospel of the kingdom.

The question is not "Should the disciples be forgiven?" but "Should we?" We have what they lacked: the clear teaching of Scripture and two thousand years of successes and failures to learn from in this matter of money. No follower of Christ today should find himself or herself living within the stronghold of "the more, the holier."

Defenses against the Stronghold

Mae West said, "I've been rich and I've been poor . . . believe me, rich is better." A lot of Christians would say amen to that, thinking, *Even if money isn't a sign of God's blessing, it will at least make me comfortable while I'm unhappy.*

That's the theory the world is promoting, and we're given plenty of opportunities to test it out. At one time I had an envelope in my desk filled with seventeen credit cards sent by banks and other institutions—all of them unsolicited. Altogether

I had been given about $400,000 of "free money" to use any way I pleased. Even if the money didn't make me happy, it would have at least made me comfortable while I figured out how to pay it all back (along with the 17-to-20-percent charges).

If you have bought into the stronghold that God wants you to be rich, there will be no end of people ready to help your dreams come true. They just won't be there to hold your hand during the bankruptcy, divorce, or other sad results that often accompany such ill-advised efforts to achieve the good life.

So how do we avoid the entrapment of Satan? How do we keep even two stones from being stacked together in the foundation of the stronghold he wants to erect in our minds? There are five ways—and they all center on the theme of contentment.

1. Be content with life's basics. Did you hear about the mother and son who lived in a forest? One day a strong tornado surprised them. The mother grabbed her son and clung to a tree, but the fierce winds tore him loose. Her son was gone. She began to weep and pray: "Please, Lord, bring back my boy! He's all I have. I'll do anything not to lose him. If You'll bring him back, I'll serve You the rest of my life." Suddenly, the wind ceased and the child fell from the sky right at his mother's feet. He was a bit rumpled, but otherwise none the worse for wear. His mother joyfully hugged him and straightened his clothes then looked carefully at her son. Turning her eyes back toward heaven, she said, "He had a hat, Lord."

Do we sometimes live like that ungrateful mother—not content with the blessings we have, always wanting more? If we do, then we are candidates for the apostle Paul's words in 1 Timothy 6:6–8: "But godliness with contentment is great gain. For we brought nothing into this world, and it is certain we can carry nothing out. And having food and clothing, with these we shall be content." We come into this world with nothing and spend all our lives accumulating stuff—all of which we will leave behind when we exit this world. Having worked in a funeral home as a teenager, I can attest to the fact that hearses do not have bumper hitches for pulling U-Haul trailers. We go, but the stuff stays.

The word *contentment* carries with it the idea of sufficiency—"enoughness." I don't know many people who could be content, like Paul wrote, with just food and clothing. It has taken me many years of walking with the Lord to reach an important conclusion about contentment: whatever God has provided in my life at any given moment needs to be enough. If I am making $30,000 per year, the answer to my discontent is not to be making $40,000. As soon as I reach that level, I will see $50,000 as the place at which I will finally be happy.

That kind of thinking is evidence of spiritual warfare—a stronghold regarding money. Paul says as much when he continues: "But those who desire to be rich fall into temptation and a snare, and into many foolish and harmful lusts which drown men in destruction and perdition. For the love of money is a root of all kinds of evil" (1 Tim. 6:9–10).

Note the five things Paul says will happen when we love money. First, we fall into temptation. Second, we fall into a snare—that's the stronghold that believes money will make us blessed and happy. Third, we are consumed by "foolish lusts." Fourth, we wander from the faith. Fifth, we are pierced with "many sorrows." None of those things will happen if we tear down the stronghold that equates money with blessedness and learn to live in a state of "enoughness."

2. Be content with gain. One of the most fascinating parables Jesus told—one that goes against all our American sensibilities of fair play—is found in Matthew 20. It's the parable where, at the end of the workday, all the workers received the same pay regardless of what time they started work. Those who had worked the longest thought they should be paid more than those who worked fewer hours. The landowner, however, rebuked them for their envy: didn't he have the right to do what he wanted with his own money?

Three lessons about work and gain are in the parable. First, if we are paid what we are promised, then we are treated justly. Someone else getting paid the same fee for serving less time is irrelevant. Second, the one who has hired you is sovereign. It is his money and he is free to strike any bargain and pay any rate that he chooses. Fairness is not part of the discussion where sovereignty is the subject, since a sovereign can do as he pleases. In theory, employers are sovereign—they can run their businesses as they see fit (at least as far as government regulations will let them).

Finally, the last lesson is not to get caught up in envy. It's easy for school teachers, policemen, and firemen to look around and wonder why media stars and professional athletes are paid a hundred times more than they are. After the September 11, 2001, terrorist attacks in which so many firefighters and policemen lost their lives, there was a lot of discussion about values and priorities—why the true heroes in our country are the most underpaid. Those who are underpaid must live with their career choices without succumbing to envy.

If we view the landowner in Jesus' parable as God, then the lessons for the Christian—especially about envy—go straight to the heart. Envy is a snare. It is our private or public testimony against the goodness and generosity of God. And remember: spiritual warfare is all about Satan working in our lives to give us reason to complain about God's nature and character. The moment we begin to complain about our lot in life—especially when fueled by envy—we enter into the throes of spiritual warfare. Envy is nothing more than discontent, wishing that our neighbor's green grass was growing on our side of the fence.

God is not against ambition and bettering oneself—unless the reasons are envy and discontent. In Proverbs, God commends industriousness and warns against being lazy (6:6–11). If you seek greater gain, make sure you allow God and your employer to be sovereign and don't accuse either of injustice because of your envy.

3. Be content with your gifts. You're at a small potluck dinner party when a couple comes through the front door and the husband drops the tuna casserole on the slate foyer floor. Now there's tuna casserole all over the foyer as well as on the feet and legs of several guests. Each guest has a different response. The person with the gift of mercy puts an arm around the husband and tells him not to worry about it. The hostess, with the gift of administration, begins assigning cleanup tasks. The prophet in the group starts to draw a spiritual analogy until his wife pokes him. The person with the gift of teaching examines the slate floor and points out how the edge of one stone is sticking up slightly—probably what caused the stumble. And the person with the gift of giving volunteers to run out and get a bucket of chicken to replace the lost tuna casserole.

See what's happening? Every person in the body of Christ has a gift or gifts given by God, and those gifts serve as motivating factors for life. Every Christian looks at life through his or her gift-colored glasses. A problem arises when we decide we would prefer other gifts than the ones God has given us.

In Romans 12:3, Paul exhorts the church "to think soberly, as God has dealt to each one a measure of faith." "Think soberly" means to think correctly, using careful judgment about our gifts. We aren't to think too highly or too lowly about ourselves in light of the spiritual gifts we have. They are, after all, a measure of the grace of God. We don't bring our gifts to God; rather, He brings them to us. That's what a gift is—something we receive. Therefore, to think too much or too little of those gifts is to impugn the judgment of God. He gave us the gifts He wants us to have, and we should use them according to His plan and purpose.

Christians can be as envious of a brother's or sister's spiritual gift as the most materialistic non-Christian can be of a wealthy person's money. Envy is as sinful inside the church as it is outside the church. And Satan will use it just as readily to attempt to make God look bad.

4. Be content with your calling. Dr. Martin Luther King Jr. made many memorable statements in his shortened life, but none so apropos to our topic as this: "If a man is called to be a street-sweeper, he should sweep streets even as Michelangelo painted, or Beethoven played music, or Shakespeare wrote poetry. He should sweep streets so well that all the hosts of heaven and earth will pause to say, 'Here lived a great street-sweeper who did his job well.'"

Paul's words in 1 Corinthians 7 about calling are well illustrated by Dr. King's words. Paul said to be content with your calling; don't think you need to change things just because change is possible. There is value and worth in being in the exact place to which God has called you. Paul used three illustrations to make his point.

First, don't feel compelled to change your spiritual status. He told the Gentile Corinthians not to undergo circumcision just because Jewish believers were circumcised. Don't look at your spiritual neighbors and try to be like them when you are from an entirely different background. Merit with God is because of Christ, not because of external trappings.

Second, don't feel compelled to change your social status. In Corinth that meant that if you were a slave when you became a Christian, be content to remain a slave. It's fine if you become a freed man, but don't think it makes any difference to God. Become a slave of Christ and you will experience all the freedom you need.

Third, don't feel compelled to change your spousal status. If you are single, don't obsess about getting married. And if you're married, don't obsess about living the single life again (v. 27). Paul says it's fine if you do decide to marry—but don't think it's the key to your spiritual happiness. And if you are married, devote your energy to taking care of the spouse you have.

Paul's point is this: we are a people on a mission. Four times he exhorts the Corinthians to remain as they are in life (vv. 17, 20, 24, 26). Why? "For the form of this world is passing away" (v. 31). "This world is not our home," the old spiritual says. "We're just a'passin' through." Our mission in life is not to flit from pillar to post, seeking what will make us the happiest. As slaves of Christ our mission is to fulfill the Great Commission He gave His church (Matt. 28:18–20). If changes take place in the context of that mission, fine. But don't drop the mission for lack of focus and contentment on your part.

It's a stronghold of Satan for you to think where you could be is better than where you are. If God moves you from status A to status B, fine. But make sure it's He and not you engineering the change.

5. Be content with your purpose. When I was a young man, I had no intention of becoming a pastor. I was a thoroughly committed Christian, but I wanted to be an evangelist. Traveling all over the world and preaching to great throngs of people appealed to some part of my youthful ego. After all, I figured, Billy Graham couldn't preach forever. I would be waiting in the wings to assume his mantle.

Somehow, God never got the memo on my future plans, because He had a church in another city call me to become their pastor. Neither my wife nor I wanted to leave our home city, but we went. Then, after eight months, like Jonah fleeing from God, we went in the opposite direction. We hadn't sold our house, making it possible for us to return to our original and familiar setting, so we did. But eventually, I got God's memo: He was calling me to be a pastor, not a traveling evangelist. So we went back to where we were called and stayed there nearly forty years, retiring in 2002.

I discovered that my evangelistic desires were completely fulfilled in our church's growth. It's funny how saying yes to God's purposes always opens doors and opportunities that we would never have thought of before. Making God's purpose our purpose is the key to finding peace and satisfaction in life.

When Pontius Pilate examined Jesus on the night of His arrest, he asked Him, "Are you a king then?" I have always loved Jesus' answer: "You say rightly that I am a king. For this cause [purpose] I was born, and for this cause [purpose] I have come into the world" (John 18:37). In plain terms Jesus was offering testimony to His God-given purpose in life: He came into this world to be the King and to proclaim the truth. There was no ambiguity in His answer at all.

If someone asked you about your current role in life, relative to purpose, how would you answer? If you don't know your purpose, or you're not happy with the purpose God has given you (like I wasn't for a while), you are providing grist for Satan's warfare mill. What kind of shepherd must God be if He allows His sheep to wander aimlessly across the pastures of this world without purpose or direction? Our lack of knowledge of or contentment with God's purpose for our life does not speak well of God.

God's call implies a purpose. Walking joyfully in your purpose instead of wishing you could walk in someone else's is the recipe for contentment.

From what I have read, I believe Jim Bakker would agree with all five of the defenses against Satan's attacks I've outlined in this chapter. And lest we smugly think nothing such as happened to him could ever happen to us, consider this: Martin Luther, the instigator of the Protestant Reformation, struggled with contentment (as do we all): "Next to faith this is the highest art—to be content with the calling in which God has placed you. I have not learned it yet." I know of no one who has completely learned it, and thus Satan continues his attack.

May you walk in contentment with the provision God has made for your life as you pursue His gain, gifts, calling, and purpose.

Discussion Questions

1. Explain the difference between God's centripetal (Old Testament) economy and His centrifugal (New Testament) economy. What impact does this difference have on notions of prosperity?

2. Have you arrived at a functional place concerning prosperity as a Christian? Or is prosperity a source of struggle and tension? Describe how you currently decide how much is enough.

3. What guidelines have you established for how much to give away and how much to keep of your money? Have you seen any connection over the years between your giving and your blessing?

4. Write a definition of contentment in your own words. How content are you with living according to that definition?

5. With how many of the five things mentioned in this chapter are you truly content: life's basics, gain, gifts, calling, and purpose? What effect have you found discontent to have on your life?

Chapter Nine

LETTING GO OF THE PAST

1 Kings 2

AN ANNUAL RITUAL FOR ME is sitting down with my appointment book at the year's end and reviewing the previous twelve months. By the time I review 365 days of appointments, meetings, events, and things done and undone—and make notes on a clean sheet of paper as I read—I have an agenda for myself: matters which require closure before I can move confidently and with a clear conscience into the new year.

I am always amazed at how many things I have forgotten by year's end. And I wonder what would happen to all this unresolved clutter had I not gone back and exhumed it from my calendar. Actually, I can tell you what would happen to the clutter. Every unresolved issue would surface again at a most inopportune time. I would see someone whom I had intended to talk with about their spiritual life and feel a twinge of conscience that I never did. I would try to avoid a person for whom I never provided the accountability I promised. Or the sight of a person with whom I had a conflict would bring up anger, proving I never really forgave.

Frankly, I would do well to go through this exercise at the end of every month. But at least every 365 days, when the new year looms, I know I have a chance to make amends and satisfy my conscience. Just writing those words makes me wince at the thought of entering a new year with those things left undone.

In this context, I am reminded of the majestic words of the General Confession found in the Episcopal *Book of Common Prayer*: "We have left undone those things which we ought to have done; and we have done those things which we ought not to have done; and there is no health in us." How much ill-health is there in the world—spiritually, emotionally, physically—because of people not resolving issues in their past? Quite a lot, I fear.

In his book *The 22 Non-Negotiable Laws of Wellness*, Greg Anderson describes how both he and a co-worker, with whom he had an unresolved conflict, were diagnosed with cancer. Given thirty days to live, he talked with everyone he could to find help. The one message that God kept communicating clearly to him was forgiveness. He knew his critical spirit and resentfulness toward his coworker had to be dealt with. He finally admitted there was a "link between [his] toxic behavior and the onset of [his] illness."

He spent four days compiling a list of people he needed to forgive and did so from his hospital bed. But his enemy at work was one he had to deal with in person. He went to the man's home and managed to tell him, "I have come to say I am sorry. I deeply regret the hurt I have caused you." His adversary replied in kind, and the two men embraced and wept together. A decade later Anderson was alive and well, a health crusader and author who still identifies the week of forgiveness as being the "absolute turning point" in his physical healing.

Think of the battleground our past can become in terms of spiritual warfare. Guilt, resentment, anger, bitterness, unforgiveness—do you see any places in that list where Satan might gain a foothold and slowly begin to tear down your spiritual defenses? Regular "housekeeping" can clean up the loose ends of our lives and slam the door on our enemy when he seeks entrance into our lives. Sometimes there are things we can't fix or can't change. At that point, we simply have to let them go, learn to cover them with God's grace, and move on.

David is the best example in Scripture, that I know, of someone who collected the loose ends of his life. When he was about to die, David turned over the throne of Israel to his son Solomon, charging Solomon with four tasks to be carried out after David's death (1 Kings 2). In these four charges, we find a paradigm to follow in our own lives for how to bring the curtain down on the past and raise the curtain on the future.

The Charge to Walk in God's Ways (1 Kings 2:2–4)

At first glance we might wonder what David's first charge to Solomon has to do with David bringing closure to his own life: "Be strong, therefore, and prove yourself a man. And keep the charge of the LORD your God: to walk in His ways, to keep His statutes, His commandments, His judgments, and His testimonies, as it is written in the Law of Moses, that you may prosper in all that you do and wherever you turn" (vv. 2–3).

That's the charge: Solomon, obey God. But the reason for the charge comes in verse 4: "That the LORD may fulfill His word which He spoke concerning me, saying, 'If your sons take heed to their way, to walk before Me in truth with all their heart and with all their soul, . . . you shall not lack a man on the throne of Israel.'"

Solomon himself was proof of the mercy and grace of God, being the fruit of David's sin-stained relationship with Bathsheba. In spite of David failing to always walk in God's ways, his son was still allowed to inherit the throne from David. But there was no promise from God that sin would always be forgiven. It hadn't been in Saul's life (1 Sam. 15), but it was in David's. Would it be in Solomon's life? The safest way for Solomon to remain on the throne of Israel was not to presume upon God's grace but to walk obediently in God's ways.

This charge to Solomon was David's way, at the end of his life, of confessing that it is far better to walk obediently with God than to test God's patience and grace. For God's promise to David to be fulfilled—that his descendants would rule on the throne of Israel—Solomon must obey God. At the end of his life David holds Solomon accountable for the future spiritual and theocratic prosperity of the nation.

There are five dimensions to Solomon's walk in obedience with God. First, Solomon was to "walk in His ways" (v. 3). The Hebrew word here (*derek*) refers to a well-trodden path, the way of God. Second, Solomon was to keep God's statutes—His decreed limits or boundaries. The ten basic boundaries for man were given by God to Moses, the first of which Solomon failed when he allowed his wives' idols to become part of Israel's worship (1 Kings 11:1–8).

Third, Solomon was to keep God's commandments—His laws. Fourth, he must keep God's judgments—what God says is right and wrong—to bring about justice in the land. And finally, he must keep God's testimonies—His warnings and repeated admonitions as passed down through generations of God's people and "written in the Law of Moses."

These admonitions to Solomon served as a way for David to summarize what he believed. It was a way for him to look back over his own life and say, "If I had it to do over again I wouldn't have shed so much blood (1 Chron. 28:3). I wouldn't have committed adultery with Bathsheba. I wouldn't have ordered the murder of her husband, Uriah. I would have spared myself the agony of a guilty conscience (Ps. 32) and the pain of confession and repentance (Ps. 51). Solomon, learn from my mistakes. Walk in God's ways 'that you may prosper in all that you do and wherever you turn.'"

When is the last time you took stock of what you believe? When I look back over my calendar at the end of a year, I see that a hundred or more times that year I proclaimed and declared the Word of God as faithfully as I knew how. I counseled scores of people from the open pages of Scripture. I see the records of daily quiet times and devotional readings. I am reminded of the hours spent in personal prayer and see the answers that came from God, not the least of which are His words of forgiveness for the times I have failed. I look in my checkbook and see evidence of an open hand as I consistently released significant portions of my resources into the hands of others to accomplish God's work in this earth. And I see the records of God's faithfulness: answered prayer, health and welfare, family and friendships, and the deep satisfaction of a soul lived in union with God.

Reviewing the past and bringing closure where needed denies Satan any foothold into my life. It reconfirms in my own mind and heart what I believe and Whom I have believed.

The Charge to Levy Justice (1 Kings 2:5–6)

Years ago there was a Fram oil filter commercial on tele vision that coined a slogan that has far outlived the company's identity: "You can pay me now or you can pay me later." That's the way it is with God's justice—it will be served, either now or later.

David failed to act justly toward a man in his employ—Joab, a loose cannon who had murdered and taken revenge without accountability to anyone. It was a blot on David's record that he never dealt with Joab when he had the opportunity, but it is to his credit that he didn't forget about Joab's wrongdoing. David's second charge to Solomon was to balance the scales of justice with regard to Joab after the king was gone.

In his early association with David, Joab was the king's most loyal and capable military commander. He was the first to enter the Jebusite stronghold on Mt. Zion. He led David's forces in a rout of the Ammonites. He arranged for David to get credit for the defeat of Rabbah and carried out David's orders to place Uriah the Hittite in the heat of that battle so he would be killed. Joab was the one who convinced David to receive back his son Absalom after Absalom was banished for the murder of his brother Ammon. When Absalom later rebelled against his father David, it was Joab who defeated Absalom's forces, even personally killing Absalom himself. Finally, it was Joab who pursued and arranged for delivery of the head of Sheba, another rebel who led a revolt against David.

But Joab's activism lacked moral boundaries; he committed murder twice. He murdered Abner, one of David's former adversaries, because Abner had killed Joab's brother, Asahel.

And he murdered Amasa, whom David had made commander of his armies instead of Joab, following the revolt of Absalom.

Do you see why the first charge David made to Solomon was about obeying God's commands and judgments? The apostle James wrote that "whoever shall keep the whole law, and yet stumble in one point, he is guilty of all" (James 2:10). For all of Joab's loyalty to David, he was still a murderer. David, himself guilty of conspiracy to murder, had learned his lesson about letting the moral garment of the nation begin to unravel.

Therefore, David's second charge to Solomon is plain: "Do not let [Joab's] gray hair go down to the grave in peace." Everybody in the land knew who Joab was and what he had done. If Solomon showed favoritism to Joab because of how he had supported Solomon's father, it would be an open invitation to cronyism in the kingdom.

When is the last time you took a relentless look at the moral fabric of your own life and the lives of those over whom you have some shepherding responsibility—in that order? Judgment has to begin first with the household of God, meaning ourselves (1 Pet. 4:17). No speck is going to come out of our brother's eye when we allow beams to be at rest in our own. Having examined ourselves, we have to bring closure to the injustices—moral, legal, practical, spiritual, relational—of those we profess to lead and love. No pastor, father, friend, or authority who will not confront is worthy to lead in the long run.

The Charge to Be Loyal (1 Kings 2:7)

Depending on your age, you may or may not remember an all-star baseball player named Pee Wee Reese. He was the emotional leader of the Boys of Summer, the post-World War II teams fielded by the original Brooklyn Dodgers. Besides being a fabulous baseball player, he was a moral leader as well. When the league's first black baseball player, Jackie Robinson, broke into the league as a Dodger, even his hometown fans did not warmly welcome him. In one game in Brooklyn, he committed an error and was roundly booed by his own fans. Then his fellow infielder Pee Wee Reese walked over and stood by him, putting his arm around Robinson's shoulder—which immediately quieted the crowd.

What Pee Wee Reese demonstrated that day was something we don't see much of in this world of "looking out for Numero Uno": loyalty. The idea in Proverbs 18:24 that "there is a friend who sticks closer than a brother" is a long-lost concept in our day. Spouses, much less friends, think nothing of abandoning the "till death do us part" thing. Loyalty (in Hebrew, *hesed*) was the foundational idea behind God's unconditional covenants with Israel. Today loyalty seems to be more conditional among His creation.

But David was nothing if not loyal. Upon the death of Saul, and Saul's son Jonathan, David took it upon himself to seek out Jonathan's surviving child, Mephibosheth, and bring him into the protection of the king's house. Why? Because David promised Jonathan he would look after Jonathan's descendants (1 Sam. 20:14–15). And he kept his word.

We see the same characteristic of loyalty surfacing in David's latter days when he charges Solomon to "show kindness to the sons of Barzillai the Gileadite, and let them be among those who eat at your table." David is repaying Barzillai's family for kindness that the aged Barzillai showed him when Absalom's rebellion drove David out of Jerusalem (2 Sam. 17:27–29; 19:31–39).

As you look back over recent months or years in your life, is there anyone's faithfulness or kindness to you that you have allowed to go unappreciated or unrewarded? I shudder to think that there might be someone out there who thinks of me as being disloyal, self-absorbed, and greedy. The quid pro quo mentality of modern politics has so distorted the biblical idea of loyalty that we are almost afraid to demonstrate it for fear of people misinterpreting our actions; thinking we're trying to get something out of them in exchange for our generosity.

Don't let modern distortions negate ancient directives. Don't allow Satan the opportunity to tempt others with bitterness and resentment born out of your unappreciative lack of loyalty. Be that friend who sticks closer than a brother, so Satan has no room to squeeze between you and another.

The Charge to Exact Vengeance (1 Kings 2:8–9)

I hope you did a double-take when you read that heading. Exact vengeance? The three previous charges have been positive ones: walk in God's ways, carry out God's justice, and extend kindness to repay loyalty. But what we are seeing now is a crack in the character of the king.

When David fled Jerusalem under pressure from Absalom's forces, a Benjamite named Shimei made a spectacle of himself by taunting and cursing the fleeing king (2 Sam. 16). With David and his escorts on a road below, Shimei walked parallel to the road on a hillside, raining down rocks, dust, and curses on David. Shimei thought that God was paying David back, delivering his kingdom into his son Absalom's hands, for David having stolen the kingdom from Saul.

David took a providential perspective toward Shimei at the time. When one of his men volunteered to go over and separate Shimei's bellowing head from his body, David declined the offer: "Let him alone, and let him curse; for so the LORD has ordered him" (2 Sam. 16:11). But this submissive posture was not to last. It appears that once Absalom's rebellion was put down and David was restored to the throne, David never forgot Shimei's disrespect.

Instead of chalking Shimei's behavior up to fanaticism, imbalance, or anger, and letting it go, David tucked it inside a place in his heart and never got over it. And he tells Solomon to "bring [Shimei's] gray hair down to the grave with blood."

It would be a stretch, but we might excuse David's vengeance as a meting out of justice—as in Joab's case. After all, throwing rocks at and cursing the king could be interpreted as reaching out against the Lord's anointed—the very thing David refused to do to Shimei's relative, King Saul (1 Sam. 26:9, 11, 23). Unfortunately, there's more to the story and it leaves David without a judicial leg to stand on.

When it was safe for David to return to Jerusalem, and he reached the east bank of the Jordan River, Shimei approached David, bowed down before him, and repented of his sins. He threw himself on the mercy of the king, asking that his previous sins not be held against him (2 Sam. 19:18–20). Again, David's men offered to kill Shimei on the spot for having previously cursed the king, but David apparently took Shimei's repentance seriously: "'You shall not die.' And the king swore to him" (v. 23). It appears that David, perhaps out of his memory of God's forgiveness of his own adultery and murder, extended genuine forgiveness to Shimei.

Or did he? When we get to the end of David's life, we see that Shimei is still the proverbial burr under David's saddle. After apparently forgiving Shimei and swearing, in the presence of hundreds of witnesses, that the man would not be killed—David now puts out a contract on Shimei through his son Solomon. What's going on here?

What's going on is David's lack of forgiveness. He had never cut the cords that bound him to Shimei. He had not been able to let go of that chapter in his past.

I can sympathize with David. There's a part of my personality that is like a dog with a bone: pick up the bone and you pick up the dog with it. I am learning in my own old age that the better part of wisdom is to let some things go. For instance, when we visited my daughter's family on her twenty-ninth birthday, their toaster took that weekend to break down. "No problem," I said. "I'll get it going again."

But when it came time for my wife and me to return to our home, the toaster still wasn't working. Nor was it working several days later after repeated efforts on my part. Contrary to my younger years when I would have fought to preserve my pride at all costs, I pronounced the benediction over that toaster and ceremonially released it into the trash bin. Done. Gone. Finished.

Some things in life are not worth the time and energy required to hold onto them. And that is especially true of things like bitterness and resentment. How much of David's royal time had been expended in stewing over the embarrassment Shimei caused him when he was fleeing Jerusalem? One second would have been too much. The man had confessed, repented, and sought forgiveness. What more was he supposed to do?

If you have a Shimei in your life, I encourage you to treat him like my daughter's old toaster—let him go. Even if the person has not confessed and repented, you are still obligated to forgive "just as God in Christ also forgave you" (Eph. 4:32). Whether it's a family member, an exspouse, a coworker, a business partner, or a friend—cut them loose. Don't sentence yourself to a lifetime of mental recriminations, looking for the opportunity to exact vengeance. That is as sure a ticket to serious spiritual warfare as anything I can imagine. If you want your future to be prosperous, you have to let go of the past and put it right.

Reviewing David's three charges to Solomon that dealt with other people, we find two things to emulate and one to avoid when reviewing our past. First, David held Joab accountable for his actions, and we may need to do that with others in our lives. Second, David paid his debt to Barzillai. Look around and see whom you may owe a debt of kindness to and pay it while you have the chance.

Finally, what are we to do about the Shimeis in our life? They will be a ball and chain that you will drag around forever if you don't cut them loose in the same way God cut you loose from your sins. Here's what we can learn from David's failure to grant freedom and forgiveness to Shimei.

First, avoid resentment completely. A friend of mine told me about a bumper sticker he saw on the back of a Toyota truck: "I'm a Pearl Harbor Survivor." If you can pay for a truck made by your former enemy, you are free of resentment.

Second, admit the problem. Pastor Rick Warren says, "Revealing your feeling is the beginning of healing." I agree. Denial, as the comics say, is not a river in Egypt. It is the refusal to acknowledge reality. How can you get over a resentment you won't admit you have?

Third, take initiative. Go to the person to extend forgiveness and seek reconciliation. If you can't do that, go to a friend and ask for help and prayer. In other words, *do something.* Satan will do whatever he can to keep you passive when action is needed. Get in motion and God will guide your steps.

Fourth, look to the future. If you say you have forgiven a sin, then your attitudes and actions will reveal it. Forgiveness is revealed by our treatment of those whom we have forgiven. When a friend of Clara Barton reminded her of a cruelty she had suffered at the hands of an acquaintance, Clara seemed not to remember the incident. "Don't you remember what was done to you?" the person asked incredulously. "No," Clara responded, "I distinctly remember forgetting that."

In *Lee: The Last Years,* author Charles Bracelen Flood records a time following the Civil War when General Lee visited a Kentucky woman whose favorite tree had been decimated by Union artillery fire. She cried bitterly over the loss of so many limbs from the majestic tree that had stood like a sentinel on her property for generations. She waited expectantly for General Lee to sympathize with her loss and condemn the Union army. Instead, after a pause, he said, "Cut it down, my dear madam, and forget it."

That advice is more than a century old but will serve us well today. Don't give Satan an opportunity to go into your past and dredge up something that you need to deal with. Your future will only be as full as your past is empty.

Discussion Questions

1. How often do you review events of the past year? What value do you see for such an exercise in your life?

2. Are there any things you have left undone in your life—things you have been hesitant to address or deal with? What could be the possibilities for spiritual warfare if you don't bring closure to these matters?

3. Can you identify any beams in your eye that you have failed to deal with while pointing out the specks in others' eyes? Again, what are the possible opportunities for spiritual warfare if you don't deal with your own issues first?

4. What issues in your life have you been unwilling to let go of (resentments, unfulfilled dreams, etc.)? How much spiritual energy is being consumed by your unwillingness to let go—energy that could be directed elsewhere?

5. Respond to the closing statement of this chapter: "Your future will only be as full as your past is empty."

IN HIS BOOK *THE JESUS I NEVER KNEW,* Philip Yancey mentions a friend whose grandmother is buried in the cemetery of an old Episcopal church in rural Louisiana. Such a graveyard scene conjures images of 150-year-old live oak trees with their massive, moss-laden branches spreading down to the ground—a place where little or nothing happens on a daily basis. It is that scene that makes the inscription on the grandmother's tombstone so appropriate: "Waiting."

That was the word the grandmother wanted on her stone—not because of the quiet setting of the cemetery, but because it expressed her theology. She was waiting on the day when Jesus would come for her and tie a knot around all the loose ends of life.

Yancey goes on to explain how our lives are like Saturday—the day with no name. We know Good Friday and we know Easter Sunday, but what of the day in between? What the disciples of Jesus experienced for twenty-four hours, we experience our entire lifetime—caught in limbo between promise and fulfillment. And we're powerless to do anything about it. Think of the utter frustration and despair the disciples must have felt that Sabbath Saturday. Their Master was in the tomb and they had no expectation that they would see Him again. I can imagine Peter, the impetuous one of the bunch, racking his brain to figure out how to jump-start the situation they were in. When the others looked at him, all he could say was, "I've got nothing. I don't know what to do."

If we're living a Saturday kind of life on a cosmic scale—waiting for Jesus to return and make everything right—we also discover it's Saturday at given times in our personal lives—*wishing* Jesus would make everything right. In the middle of heated battles, we find ourselves uttering (and hopefully praying) Peter-like words: "I've got nothing, Lord. I don't know what to do."

The founder of the famous cosmetics empire, Estée Lauder, found herself in a waiting mode one day. She had just started her business and needed to persuade a certain cosmetics buyer to begin placing Lauder products in stores throughout the county. So at 9:00 a.m. she entered the offices of the American Merchandising Corporation to see a Ms. Weston, the cosmetics buyer. Not having made an appointment, Lauder was advised to come back another day.

"I don't mind waiting," the entrepreneur said, and took a seat.

At noon, the receptionist again advised her to return another day—that the buyer's schedule was so packed it would be impossible to see her.

"I'll wait a little longer," Lauder said.

At 5:15 p.m. Ms. Weston appeared in the waiting area and looked at Estée Lauder in disbelief, then admiration. "Well, do come in," she said. "Such patience must be rewarded."

In time, space was found in a few stores for the Estée Lauder products, and the rest is business history.

The day that patient, persistent woman spent sitting—waiting—in a receptionist's space is not unlike the time we spend waiting while God fights for us. Lauder knew that behind closed doors, things were happening; a manager's to-do list was being whittled down so that eventually there would be room for her to be seen. We have to believe that behind heaven's closed doors, God is doing His thing, and we must wait. We have to agree that there are some things only God can do.

The battle is always the Lord's. There are times when we have specific things to do, such as clothe ourselves in spiritual armor (Eph. 6). And there are other times when there is nothing we can do, as in Jehoshaphat's case, beyond casting one's self on the Lord. "O our God, wilt thou not judge them? For we have no might against this great company that cometh against us; neither know we what to do: but our eyes are upon thee" (2 Chron. 20:12 KJV). In either situation, the battle is the Lord's.

In this chapter I want to focus on those times when we are called to wait and watch while the Lord fights for us—doing those God things that only He can do. It is not easy for activist American Christians to let someone else do the heavy lifting, but that is what we are called to do at times in spiritual warfare.

God works in this world to do battle for us in seven ways—seven instances when He says, "Stop striving. Stand and watch what I am going to do." Nothing shocks us back into the reality that life is all about God—not all about us—than being helpless in matters of warfare. I remember being hit by that spiritual two-by-four when I read John Owen's *The Death of Death in the Death of Christ.* As the Puritans were wont to do, he clearly explains why Christianity is completely God-centered, not man-centered. I believe God allows us to get into situations in which we are helpless to demonstrate that He is not.

God Can Defy Natural Laws

A May 1, 2000 *Newsweek* magazine poll revealed some interesting facts about what Americans believe:

- Percentage of Americans who believe in divine miracles: 84
- Percentage who believe in the reality of miracles described in the Bible: 79
- Percentage who have personal experiences with miracles: 48
- Percentage who know of people who have personal experience with miracles: 63
- Percentage who have prayed for a miracle: 67
- Percentage who believe God or the saints cure or heal sick people who have been given no chance of survival by medical doctors: 77

It's a good thing that poll wasn't taken among the Hebrew slaves who followed Moses out of Egypt. In spite of having just witnessed ten of the most amazing disruptions of the laws of nature known in history, they thought they were doomed when they saw the Red Sea in front of them and the Egyptian army behind them. What could they do—float across the sea in their cooking pots? Throw their newly acquired gold and silver at the approaching warriors? This was a classic case of "If God doesn't do something, we're goners."

The people were crying out to Moses, and Moses was crying out to God. Moses was on the right track when he told the people, "Stand still, and see the salvation of the LORD. . . . The LORD will fight for you" (Exod. 14:13–14). But God rebuked Moses and told him to cut out the talking and crying and to get moving (verse 15). I love that. God says, "Enough praying already! Just listen to what I tell you to do and you'll be delivered."

You know the story: Moses stretched out his rod over the waters, the waters parted, and the people walked through on dry ground. And when the Egyptians tried to get in on the miracle, they were drowned.

In spite of the bold professions of the American populace, something tells me a lot of people would give a wink and a nod to that story. Scientific humanism and materialism, in which we are all steeped, has little room for defying the laws of nature. But Moses said it happened, and he ought to know. He was there when it happened, and he wrote it down. He brought a wooden stick to the battle, and God brought everything else.

I would never predict when and where God might choose to defy the laws of nature to win a battle for you. I only know that He has for some and He can for you.

God Can Destroy Natural Materials

When Andy Griffith, star of the beloved TV show that bore his name, hit his fifties, he hit a brick wall professionally. No one wanted to hire him to act. And things were getting harder financially by the day. He wrote in *Guideposts* that he and his wife, Cindi, decided things would be easier if they moved back to Andy's home state of North Carolina. But their California house sat on the market for months without a decent offer.

One day Cindi said that maybe the house's not selling was the grace of God, keeping them in California. If they moved back to North Carolina, Andy indeed might never work again. "What we need to do is stay here and stoke the fire," she told Andy. And they did. With renewed vigor they began meeting with agents and producers, and the work began to come in: four TV movies that year, including the pilot for *Matlock*, a show that ran for nine years.

Andy Griffith's obstacles were people who didn't want to hire him. You may be facing a similar obstacle—someone who wants to fire you from your job or makes life difficult for you in other ways. Or maybe it's some other person, place, or thing that stands in your way—something impossible for you to move.

If you face such an obstacle, you have an ally in Joshua. You probably know Joshua's story too well. By that, I mean we tend to discount what God did in practical terms, putting His acts of old into the "Bible story" category. But if we take seriously what God did for Joshua, we will not hesitate to call upon Him to remove an obstacle in our path as well.

Jericho stood in the path of the Hebrews as they prepared to enter the promised land. In Joshua 6, we find the instructions God gave Joshua: march around Jericho once a day for six days. On the seventh day march around it seven times. When the priests blew the trumpets, the people were to shout and the obstacle would be removed—the walls would "come a'tumblin' down." Joshua was obedient, and the walls came down without Joshua lifting a hand. Once the walls were down, conquering Jericho was not a problem.

Don't make the mistake of thinking you need to march around your boss or your illness or your financial debts to see them removed. Don't focus on the strategy; focus on the strength of God. Learn from Joshua's example: stand back, take directions, follow them, and watch what God does.

God Can Deliver Nature's Elements

It has become common for churches to use dramas on Sunday morning to set the stage for the preaching of the Word. Back in the late 1970s, a creative church in Dallas was on the cutting edge of this movement. For one performance, the stage they set depicted an "office" in heaven where prayer requests came in from earth. Several long tables were set up with banks of telephones on them. St. Peter was in charge of answering the phones and recording the prayer requests.

One of the most thought-provoking elements from the drama was when two people from the same town called asking for the exact opposite in weather conditions for the same day. One was a farmer whose crops desperately needed rain; the other was an evangelist who needed fair skies for a giant outdoor rally. Peter was uncharacteristically speechless. How would you have responded to those prayer requests? How do you think God does?

Undoubtedly God has different purposes for the farmer and the evangelist regardless of which weather pattern develops. And He definitely had different purposes for Joshua. As the Israelites pressed on into the promised land, Joshua made a covenant with the Gibeonites to defend them, not knowing the Gibeonites were about to be attacked by a coalition of five kings. Joshua took Israel's armies up to defend Gibeon, but probably with fear and trembling. Then God sent Joshua a word: "I have delivered them into your hand; not a man of them shall stand before you" (Josh. 10:8). Of all things, God sent a hailstorm to defeat the coalition of kings. In fact, "There were more who died from the hailstones than those whom the children of Israel killed with the sword" (v. 11).

We cannot begin to fathom how God uses the natural elements in this world to accomplish His purposes—especially when one element like a flood or snowstorm serves His purposes with multitudes of different people. But whenever I see rain or snow, or worse, I think of Joshua and how God used the movements of nature to fight and win a battle for him. Don't hesitate to ask God to move nature for you if it can win a battle you're fighting. He's the only one who can, and the only one who will.

God Can Destroy Perceptions

If I mention the name John Wayne to you, what image comes to mind? Usually, it's the gun-slingin', maiden-rescuin', bad-guy-kickin' macho man of the wild West.

But did you know that the man who lionized the Green Berets in Vietnam actually got out of World War II so he could focus on acting? That the man who looked like he was born on a horse actually hated horses? And the man who acted like he used tumbleweed for a pillow and cactus thorns for toothpicks was born in Iowa and given the genteel-sounding name of Marion Morrison? And in this day of digital deception, it's getting increasingly difficult to be sure that who or what we see is actually the real who or what.

God is in the business of changing perceptions, and the story of Gideon's victory over the Midianites in Judges 6–7 is a good illustration of how. Three different perceptions were at work in this instance. First, Gideon perceived himself to be the weakest man in the weakest clan in the tribe of Manasseh—and, in the flesh, he might have been. Second, Gideon probably perceived the narrowed-down force of three hundred soldiers God gave him as being far too few to defeat the Midianites. And finally, the Midianites likely perceived Gideon and his forces to be too weak to defeat them (until God gave one Midianite a dream in which their defeat was foretold).

As it turned out, all three perceptions were wrong. The result was a great victory for Gideon and Israel. Gideon turned out to have just what the Lord needed: faithfulness. He gave Gideon a strategy for deploying the three hundred that made them appear like thousands to the Midianites. And the Midianites fled when God gave them a new perception of how numerous the Israelites were. Simply by altering perceptions, one weak man led three hundred soldiers to defeat thousands.

The lesson is this: *never* judge the potential for victory based on your five senses. What God may do in the spiritual realm—which your five senses will completely miss—can alter the entire outcome of the battle you're in. But altering perceptions is something only God can do. Our job is to walk by faith, not by sight (2 Cor. 5:7).

God Can Disrupt Hearing

In *Character Forged from Conflict*, Gary Preston tells a story of a young man who answered a newspaper ad for a Morse code operator at the local telegraph office. He filled out the application and took a seat with the other applicants waiting to be interviewed. Presently he rose and entered the office without being summoned, then reappeared a few moments later with the interviewer. The interviewer thanked the other applicants for coming in and dismissed them, announcing that the young man had filled the position. When the other applicants' objected, the interviewer said, "All the time you've been sitting here, the telegraph has been ticking out this message: 'If you understand this message, then come right in. The job is yours.' None of you heard or understood the message. This young man did, so the job is his."

That young man heard something that no one else did, and he got a job. On one occasion in the Old Testament, God saved Israel from her attackers by causing the enemy army to hear something no one else heard. In their case, it's because there was no actual noise. But God filled their ears with sounds that caused them to flee.

The army of Syria had besieged Samaria, the capital of the northern kingdom of Israel. People in Samaria were starving—even eating their own children to stay alive. They were completely helpless to save themselves. However, when a group of lepers wandered into the Syrian camp, they found it deserted—the entire army had fled in great haste. After eating their fill of the Syrians' food and stashing some of their gold and silver, the lepers went to the gates of Samaria and told the people that the Syrians had fled—and the city was saved.

Why did the Syrian army flee? Because "the LORD had caused the army of the Syrians to hear the noise of chariots and the noise of horses—the noise of a great army; so they said to one another, 'Look, the king of Israel has hired against us the kings of the Hittites and the kings of the Egyptians to attack us!' Therefore they arose and fled at twilight, and left the camp intact—their tents, their horses, and their donkeys—and they fled for their lives" (2 Kings 7:6–7).

Many people consume themselves and their families out of fear—without remembering that God can cause enemies to flee. Whatever situation or circumstance you are facing, God is perfectly capable of fighting for you—and winning—without your doing a thing. You may have to open your city gate and go out and claim the victory by faith. But that's not too much to ask after God has won the victory, is it?

God Can Deal Death

Everyone has heard actor Woody Allen's famous line about death: "It's not that I'm afraid to die. I just don't want to be there when it happens." Ha! As if we had anything to say about the timing of that last great event. Solomon wrote in Ecclesiastes that there is a "time to be born, and a time to die; a time to plant, and a time to pluck what is planted" (3:2). Life and death are in God's hands, along with everything else in this world (Pss. 31:15; 139:16).

That's why God was free to use death when He fought for Israel during the reign of Hezekiah. This time Jerusalem was surrounded by the Assyrians—scores of thousands of them. The Assyrians had been mocking God, asking Hezekiah where the gods of the other nations were when Assyria conquered them. There was no way Israel could defeat the savage Assyrians, so Hezekiah turned to God. Through Isaiah the prophet,

God delivered a word of comfort to the king: "I will defend this city, to save it for My own sake and for My servant David's sake" (2 Kings 19:34).

The next morning Israel discovered the bodies of 185,000 Assyrian soldiers lying dead in the fields around Jerusalem. No word is given on how they died—only that they did. And Sennacherib, the king of Assyria, retreated.

Now, don't misinterpret my use of death as an example for you and whatever battle you find yourself in. Your prayer to God should be the same as Hezekiah's: "O LORD our God, I pray, save us from his hand, that all the kingdoms of the earth may know that You are the LORD God, You alone" (2 Kings 19:19). Hezekiah didn't pray for 185,000 people to be killed. Rather, he prayed for deliverance for the purpose of the glory of God.

I cite this example, gruesome as it is, to remind you yet again that God is in charge. "The world is mine, and all that is in it," God says (Ps. 50:12 NIV). However God chooses to fight is His call, not ours. God can use any means to cause your enemies—be they people, places, or things—to break camp and withdraw from the fight. Leave the means to God. You pray, stand, and watch so you don't miss what He does.

God Can Divide the Enemy

Among the many fables told by Aesop is the story of the father with quarreling sons. The father cured their dissension by demonstrating how none of them was able to break a bundle of sticks tied together, but that individual sticks could easily be snapped in two. "United we stand, divided we fall" was the moral of that story.

Israel's enemies—those from Ammon, Moab, and Mount Seir—could have profited from this demonstration when they gathered themselves in a coalition against Jerusalem. Jehoshaphat, the king in Israel, went before the Lord and said, "[The intruders are] coming to throw us out of Your possession which You have given us to inherit. O our God . . . we have no power against this great multitude that is coming against us; nor do we know what to do, but our eyes are upon You" (2 Chron. 20:11–12).

And that is the summary of this chapter: we have no power to fight our battles, but God does. All we can do is lay our case out before God and wait and watch. Never in a thousand years would Jehoshaphat have expected to see the thing God did. First, the armies of Ammon and Moab turned on the armies of Mount Seir and destroyed them. Then they turned on each other and routed one another. Done—battle over. God divided Israel's enemies and they turned on each other. God rescued His people when He was their only resource.

Maybe a coalition of people have ganged up on you. Or there may be a confluence of people, places, and things—money, men, circumstances—in a confederacy about to overwhelm you. If you will confess your dependence on the Lord and put your eyes totally on Him, you will see what He does. I doubt if He will do for you exactly what He did for Jehoshaphat. Again, don't focus on the means. Focus on God's ability to see you through.

These seven examples from God's dealings with His people in trouble tempt us to want God to do the same dramatic things for us that He did for others. But rarely did God do the same dramatic thing twice. Instead of focusing on the drama, focus on the deity and His deliverance—and try the following steps.

1. Remember to wait. Do everything you know to do that is required of you—examine yourself, give thanks in all things, remain in prayer—and then stand still. Sometimes you will have to wait during that Saturday time Philip Yancey talked about. But be obedient and wait.

2. Remember how big you aren't. I know it's not the American way, but you have to be willing to say, "This battle is bigger than I am. I've done all I know to do. I admit I am helpless in this setting." It's OK—you've just read about some pretty significant people who had to say the same thing.

3. Remember whose you are. In this world God has always done whatever it took to preserve a remnant of people for His glory and His purposes. He has not forgotten you. Rest in the fact that as His child, you are secure in His arms.

4. Remember who's taking the risk. When you stand still and wait on God and confess your dependence on Him, it's His name at stake, not yours. The question is not whether He is willing to risk His name in fighting for you—it's whether you are.

Growing up, my five brothers and I stuck together. I remember losing a fist fight in the eighth grade, and when I got home my older brother John was ready to go find my assailant and fight for me. We have an older brother in the faith, Jesus of Nazareth, who stands ready at the right hand of God to come to our defense and fight for us. He intercedes for us, pleads our case before the Father, and looks out for those battles we can't win without His direct intervention. Stick with Him and you will be saved in all things.

Discussion Questions

1. How many times in your life have you prayed for God to do something outside the laws of nature? How much faith do you have to continue praying that way when you are in need?

2. How do you approach the miracles in the Bible—especially those instances when people were delivered from destruction by a miracle? Should you expect God to deliver His people the same way today? Explain.

3. What experience have you had with feeling inadequate about something to which God was calling you? What did you do? How did you change the perception?

4. Respond to and explain this statement from the chapter: "Never judge the potential for victory based on your five senses." On what should you judge the potential for victory?

5. Have you or your family members ever found your backs against the wall—no resources, no outlets, no way to survive a given situation? Where did crying out to God for His deliverance fall in whatever steps you ultimately took? To what degree do you look at God as one who can rescue you when all else fails?

Chapter Eleven

WINNING AT SPIRITUAL WARFARE

Joshua 22:1–10

THE DECISION WEIGHING ON THE MIND of Dwight D. Eisenhower, supreme commander of the Allied forces in World War II, was difficult: Should he launch the planned D-Day invasion on June 5, 1944, in spite of terrible weather? Or postpone the invasion for one day in hopes the weather would clear? Or postpone the launch for two weeks, the next time the moon and tides would be optimum, and risk giving German forces more time to mount their defense?

When the top American and British generals met on June 2 to review the plan, the weather forecast for June 5 was for sheeting rain and heavy seas—not good weather for thousands of ships and tens of thousands of troops to cross the English Channel. When military meteorologists forecast a slight break in the inclement weather for June 6, Eisenhower made the call: D-Day would be June 6, 1944. And so it was. An invasion force of four thousand ships, eleven thousand planes, and nearly three million soldiers lumbered into action. Nearly 160,000 troops entered Europe on the beaches and from the sky over France. Thus was set in motion the ultimate defeat of the Axis powers led by Germany.

On June 11, General Eisenhower pulled from his wallet a note he had written on June 5 and showed it to his aide, Harry C. Butcher. The note read, "Our landings in the Cherbourg-Havre area have failed to gain a satisfactory foothold and I have withdrawn the troops. My decision to attack at this time and place was based upon the best information available. The troops, the air, and the Navy did all that bravery and devotion to duty could do. If any blame or fault attaches to the attempt, it is mine alone."

Eisenhower told his aide that he had written a similar contingency note for every amphibious operation in the war but had always destroyed them once the operation succeeded. Butcher asked if he might keep the one written for D-Day and include it in the general's diaries, and Eisenhower agreed.

This was not the only note Eisenhower wrote in the fading hours of June 5, after giving the order for the invasion to begin on June 6. He also wrote a note, to be used as a press release, acknowledging victory and giving credit to everyone who had participated in the successful invasion. This is the note that was released to the public—but not immediately. We see from the record that it took six days for him to decide to take the "defeat" note out of his wallet and (almost) tear it up.

Eisenhower knew that every war can have two outcomes—and wars hang in the balance for a period of time until the outcome is certain. The same is true in spiritual warfare at the personal level. At God's level, we know that Satan is a defeated foe.

At our level, however, he still is making war against God, using us as his targets.

The Swiss theologian Oscar Cullman, who lived during World War II, pointed out that every military campaign in history has had a decisive battle. For Napoleon, it was Waterloo. For the Confederates, it was Gettysburg. And in World War II it was the Normandy invasion—D-Day. In spiritual warfare, the turning point came in the three-day battle that began in Gethsemane and ended at the empty garden tomb. Christ put sin to death on the cross and conquered death in the resurrection. Satan's fate was sealed at the end of that seventy-two-hour span, just as the fate of the Axis powers was sealed by the D-Day invasion. Yet history records that death and destruction rage on even after a key battle has been fought. In the battles following D-Day, more Allied soldiers died than in the invasion itself.

And so it goes in spiritual warfare. Though the outcome of the campaign is sure, the outcome of every individual skirmish hangs in the balance for a period of time—minutes, hours, days, perhaps years—while we wrestle at the spiritual level. For that reason it is imperative that we arm ourselves for victory. We know that attacks will come until the day Jesus Christ returns and proclaims a spiritual V-Day for the people of God.

Spiritual warfare is a spiritual conflict in heaven that is manifested in a material way on earth. Satan's attacks on God may find their battleground in a church, a marriage, a thought life, a business setting, or a relational conflict. How we respond in those settings is a function of our obedience to the commands of God—whether we respond immediately by taking His way of escape (1 Cor. 10:13) or not.

The devil's agenda in spiritual warfare is not always apparent. We may think we are initially in a benign setting and suddenly find ourselves in the midst of full-blown spiritual warfare.

In my early days of counseling as a pastor I learned that the truth about marital situations was three-sided: the wife's view, the husband's view, and the truth. I would be pulled emotionally from one side to the other as I listened to each party separately, but quickly learned that the truth was somewhere in between. And it was my job to find it. I saw that mistaken perceptions and assumptions could lead me to become a pawn of the counselee.

It is the same in spiritual warfare. Satan's agenda is hidden. He will create perceptions and suggest assumptions that can lead to your defeat. The key to immediate victory is to stay focused on the truth and commands of God. The Word of God is alive and powerful and able to discern the thoughts and intents of the heart (Heb. 4:12).

In Joshua 22 we have an excellent example of how perceptions and assumptions can get completely out of hand and lead to serious conflict between people who were unified only moments before. If all the parties involved had taken Joshua's words to heart—"But take careful heed to do the commandment and the law which Moses the servant of the LORD commanded you, to love the LORD your God, to walk in all His ways, to keep His commandments, to hold fast to Him, and to serve Him with all your heart and with all your soul" (v. 5)—the conflict might have been avoided. Staying filled with the Spirit, Word, and wisdom of God is the only way to see through the deceitful strategies of Satan.

The Power of Perception

When the twelve tribes of Israel crossed the Jordan River and moved into Canaan to claim their inheritance, the tribes of Reuben and Gad and half the tribe of Manasseh asked permission to settle on the east side of the Jordan. Joshua granted their request on one condition: they had to accompany the rest of the tribes into Canaan and help them drive out the inhabitants before returning to their own tribal lands. Joshua 22 opens with the two-and-a-half tribes returning to the east side of the Jordan after helping their fellow Israelites claim their own territory in Canaan (v. 9).

While still in Canaan, on the west bank of the Jordan, the two-and-a-half tribes stopped before crossing over and built "a great, impressive altar." No word is given as to why or to whom the altar was dedicated. But when the nine-and-a-half tribes got word of what their brethren had done, "the whole congregation of the children of Israel gathered together at Shiloh to go to war against them" (v. 12). Their action was based on hearsay, not fact: "the children of Israel heard someone say" (v. 11). Before sending a delegation to the site of the altar to discover its purpose, the majority tribes gathered for war. Their perception was that the two-and-a-half tribes had already abandoned Joshua's admonitions to "walk in all [God's] ways, to keep His commandments, to hold fast to Him" (v. 5). They concluded that the altar-builders had lapsed into idolatry before even leaving the land of Israel. And they were prepared to go to war on the basis of this perception.

I had driven to a certain town for a meeting where a man issued an invitation to me: "I'd like to take you to Magnetic Hill where there is so much magnetic rock in the earth that it pulls cars up the hill." I thought he was kidding, of course, but agreed to go along for the ride. And from a certain vantage point, it appeared that what he said was true. A car, put in neutral with the motor off, would begin coasting "up" this particular hill. But it was all an illusion—an impressive one, but an illusion nonetheless. From where we stood, given the lay of the surrounding land, it did appear that the road on the hill ran upwards. In reality, however, it slanted downhill.

The power of perception, in that case, could cause the observer to see a distortion of reality. And that is what was happening with the tribes who gathered to go to war against their brethren who built an altar.

Satan loves to use perception to create conflict and dissension. How many times have you perceived something to be one way only to find out it was another? People, families, churches, and friends have all been separated—sometimes for years—on the basis of faulty perceptions.

The *New York Times* reported that in October 1997, scientists released a "photograph" taken by the Hubble space telescope. The picture was of a massive, invisible star. Labeled the Piston Star, it is located near the center of our Milky Way galaxy. It burns as brightly as 10 million of our suns and could fill up the entire space inside of earth's orbital path around the sun. However, human eyes and telescopes have never seen it because it is hidden by an impenetrable cloud of cosmic dust.

So how did the scientists get a photograph of it? In truth, the "photo" is a computer-generated image based on measurements of infrared rays that are not visible to the human eye. They are, however, detectable by instruments on the Hubble. Therefore, what we cannot see, and cameras can't record on film, a computer can draw a picture of based on the infrared rays emanating from it. So—based on perception alone, the Piston Star doesn't exist. Based on reality, it does. Based on perception, we conclude lots of erroneous things in life. Based on reality, we have to repent. Unfortunately, sometimes the damage is done before reality sets in.

You would think a star brighter than ten million suns would be plainly visible in the sky. And you would think that our minds would always see the truth. But when clouds of prejudice, bias, distortion, and preference block our senses, we end up missing something that seems painfully obvious later. Satan loves to engage us in the battlefield of the mind and entice us to put our trust in our perception.

I've said before in this book that deceived people don't know they're deceived—and I repeat that warning here. We act with such conviction on our perceptions because we can't imagine they're unreal. We ought to hold lightly everything we hear, think, and feel until we have taken it before God and asked Him to confirm it in our mind and spirit. First impressions are the last impressions we ought to put our trust in.

Back to our story: while the nine-and-a-half tribes were gearing up for war, they sent representatives from each tribe, along with a priest, to investigate. The first words out of their mouths were accusatory: "What treachery is this that you have committed against the God of Israel?" (Josh. 22:16). Not "How's it going?" or "What's up?" or "Good to see you!" or "Can we talk?" An accusation right off the bat. They were trusting in their perception of what their brethren had done.

The Act of Assumption

The transition from perception to assumption is a slow slide down the slippery slope of arrogance. We perceive, ergo we assume. Where do we get off thinking that what our five senses take in at a given moment in time encompasses all the reality there is? But in spiritual warfare, that is the encouragement that Satan offers: *Haven't you seen and heard enough? Go ahead and make your assumptions. You're on solid ground.*

Let's be clear: there's nothing wrong with confronting sin in the body of Christ—if, indeed, it is sin. The elders from the majority tribes remembered what had happened at times in Israel's past when "sin in the camp" had resulted in the whole nation's suffering. When Achan sinned, many were punished (Josh. 7). When some worshipped Baal at Peor, many died (Num. 25). The elders said, "And it shall be, if you rebel today against the LORD, that tomorrow He will be angry with the whole congregation of Israel" (Josh. 22:18).

We can't fault the committee for wanting to extinguish the spark of idolatry before it grew into a flame that consumed the nation. Their problem was that they were acting on assumptions based on perceptions.

I read a story about a woman who bought a pack of cookies in an airport to eat while she waited for her plane's departure. She settled in to read her newspaper when, to her surprise, she heard the rustling of paper. She glanced down to see the man in the seat next to her helping himself to one of her cookies from where they sat on the small table between their seats. Instead of saying something, she sought to prove that those were *her* cookies by reaching down and taking one herself. A few minutes later, more rustling! The thief was helping himself to another of her cookies. To add insult to injury, the man eventually broke the last cookie in two, pushed one half toward her, ate the other, and then left.

She was still fuming about the rudeness of this man when her flight was called. Opening her purse to get her ticket, she discovered the pack of cookies she had bought—unopened and uneaten. To such embarrassing conclusions does the arrogance of assumptions often lead.

Think of all the rifts in relationships among people you know—in families, churches, among friends, among nations. How many of them are based on false assumptions?

Fortunately, before the war started over a pile of rocks erected on the banks of the Jordan River, the truth came out.

The Clarity of Conversation

If there is one thing Satan absolutely hates, it's truth. Jesus told the religious leaders of His day that they could not understand His teachings for a reason: "You are of your father the devil, and the desires of your father you want to do. He . . . does not stand in the truth, because there is no truth in him. When he speaks a lie, he speaks from his own resources, for he is a liar and the father of it" (John 8:44). The New International Version says, "When [the devil] lies, he speaks his native language." And The Message says, "He couldn't stand the truth because there wasn't a shred of truth in him. When the Liar speaks, he makes it up out of his lying nature."

Therefore, the best way to defeat the strategies of the devil is to deal in the truth. People won't always agree about the implications of the truth—they may agree to disagree—but without having the truth as a basis in fact, assumptions will rule the day. The truth is the currency of the kingdom; it is how we transact business. If we don't agree that two plus two equals four, whatever business we transact will be as invalid as if I had paid for it with counterfeit bills.

When the elders from the majority tribes accosted the minority tribes, they weren't agreeing on the sum of two plus two. There was a pile of rocks between them—an altar—and they didn't agree on its purpose. Fortunately, even though the accusers didn't ask, the accused tribes offered a quick explanation that defused a combustible situation.

It turns out that the two-and-a-half tribes had built the altar not to compete with the tabernacle at Shiloh but out of an entirely legitimate concern. They were afraid that, generations hence, the descendants of the nine-and-a-half tribes might attempt to disown the descendants of the two-and-a-half tribes because they lived across the Jordan River. After all, it was the land of Canaan (on the west side of the Jordan) that had been initially designated as Israel's inheritance. "What if, someday, someone accuses our descendants of having no portion with the Lord because we don't live in the former land of Canaan?" the accused tribes were saying.

To keep such a misunderstanding from happening, they built a "replica of the altar of the LORD which our fathers made, though not for burnt offerings nor for sacrifices; but it is a witness between you and us" (Josh. 22:28). In other words, it was to be a memorial of a decision made by Joshua, approved by the Lord, to allow the two-and-a-half tribes to live on the east side of the Jordan River. It was a way to preserve the unity of Israel for future generations.

Oh.

That's what I imagine the elders from the majority tribes said after hearing the eloquent explanation from the leaders of Reuben, Gad, and the half-tribe of Manasseh. The majority tribes were ready to destroy the unity of Israel because of their assumptions about something the minority tribes had done to preserve that unity. Their assumptions had been totally wrong. And all it took to clarify the matter was a simple conversation. After affirming their brethren—but without an apology—the priest and elders from the majority tribes returned to Shiloh, probably complimenting themselves all the way for their preemptive strike against idolatry. I wonder if it occurred to them that they almost destroyed the unity of their nation because of their assumptions.

They might have struck first and asked questions, if ever, later—as we often do. How many times has one spouse brooded all day, nursing hurt feelings, and then unloaded on their partner that night over something they were mistaken about? The partner walks in the front door and—wham!—a surprise attack. No warning, just a verdict of guilty: "The judge and jury met while you were out and decided you are in big trouble!"

Parents, talk to your teenagers. Don't assume that because they were with a group that made poor choices that your children did the same. Husband, talk to your wife. Don't assume that the scratch on the car was her fault. Wife, talk to your husband. Don't assume he was late for a trivial reason. Pastor, talk to your board. Don't assume that the tension you have been feeling has something to do with your performance.

Satan hates it when we talk to each other because we might discover that which he cannot stand: the truth. He will do everything in his power to keep us from sitting down with one another and blowing away the fog of perception that has clouded reality.

Don't ever believe that, in spiritual matters, what you see is what you get. What you see and experience on earth should be taken as a harbinger of something that is happening in heavenly places. If you are experiencing anger or frustration or doubt or hate toward a person, stop and assess the situation for what it is: an earthly playing out of something bigger and more significant in heaven. Satan is trying to bring reproach upon God's name by stirring up carnality in your life and in your relationships. If he can divide Christian brothers and sisters at any level—in families, friendships, congregations, or communities—then he has succeeded in bringing reproach and dishonor upon the name of God Himself.

It's commendable that the situation in Joshua 22 was resolved peacefully. Unity was maintained and truth was honored. But it would have been far better if it had never gotten as far as it did. Jesus said that when we (think we) see that our brother has sinned, we are to go to him personally and discuss the matter—again with two or three others if need be. The entire church is to be involved only as a last resort (Matt. 18:15-17). The elders of the nine-and-a-half tribes did it in reverse. They told everyone first, then sent a small group of eleven people, then had Phinehas, the priest, speak for the group.

When my parents' fiftieth wedding anniversary approached, I waited to hear from one of my siblings as to what we would do to honor the occasion. Hearing nothing, and with the date approaching, I wrote a letter to my brothers and older sister and put forth some ideas for an anniversary party. My sister did not take kindly to my encroaching on what she viewed as her territory—being the oldest child and leader of the siblings—and let me know that she would take care of the planning.

After the phone lines had cooled off for a few days, I realized the devil was working on me and creating a division between my sister and me. So I wrote her a long letter, apologizing for my brusque actions in usurping what had traditionally been her role. My perception was that I didn't see any planning taking place and so assumed that my siblings either didn't care or were being lazy. So I acted on my assumptions. I told her I was wrong and apologized.

When she received my letter, she called and we talked. She too apologized for her reaction. We prayed together over the phone and put out a smoldering coal of resentment that could have set off a firestorm and ruined a glorious occasion for our parents. By speaking the truth in love to one another, we established a wall of truth around ourselves that allowed Satan no entrance. We were the victors, Satan the vanquished.

Discussion Questions

1. Explain why God allows spiritual attacks by Satan to continue even though Satan is a defeated foe whose ultimate doom is certain.

2. What are the primary distractions that occur during spiritual warfare? What are the essential spiritual elements upon which you must remain focused to be victorious?

3. Describe a time when you jumped to a conclusion based on a false perception of someone's actions. What harm resulted? What did you learn about perceptions from the experience?

4. How do we describe God's actions? Why do we need to leave room in our perceptions for His ways not being our ways before jumping to conclusions?

5. Explain the meaning of the principle that "truth is the currency of the kingdom." Why will Satan always attempt to alter the truth? How valid is relational or theological business conducted on anything but truth?

6. What are three insights you have gained from this book that can make a difference in your own spiritual battles?

IF YOU ARE GOING TO AVOID Satan's traps and be victorious in spiritual warfare—if you are going to avoid carrying two press releases around in your wallet as General Eisenhower did, one in case of victory and the other in case of defeat—you're going to have to do the following three things.

1. Stay out of the trap. Don't fall for the idea that what you perceive with your senses is all there is. This world is nothing more than an old Western movie set with the facades of buildings held up by temporary supports. Behind the facade of this world is the world of heavenly places. Don't let Satan convince you that you have things figured out based on what your five senses tell you. You have to go behind the facade to discover what you're missing by walking down the Main Streets of this world.

2. Live for the truth. Jesus said "the truth shall make you free" (John 8:32). Any relational or other business you transact based on lies—perceptions and assumptions—will not stand. You will be sorry you ever went to the store with that kind of currency.

"Speaking the truth in love" (Eph. 4:15) is the only way to get past perceptions and assumptions to reality.

3. Exercise your citizenship. Your residence is in this physical world, but your citizenship is in heaven if you are a born-again Christian (Phil. 3:20). Satan has access to both realms but is like a cur on a long leash—and the leash is held by God. Satan is not omnipotent, omniscient, or omnipresent, but he is strong and deceitful and conniving. Because you are a citizen of heaven, you are not obligated to yield to his earthly pressures. You have the option of winning every spiritual battle if you will exercise it.

Truth and love are not mutually exclusive (1 Tim. 1:5). They find their fulfillment at the foot of the cross of Christ where they are bound together in the selfless sacrifice of the Savior. Until He returns and consummates the campaign His death and resurrection has assured, may you be the ultimate, if not immediate, victor in every battle you face on this earth.